BERKLEE PRESS

Melody in Songwriting

Tools and Techniques for Writing Hit Songs

Jack Perricone

Berklee Press

Director: Dave Kusek
Managing Editor: Debbie Cavalier
Marketing Manager: Ola Frank
Sr. Writer/Editor: Jonathan Feist

ISBN 0-634-00638-X

1140 Boylston Street
Boston, MA 02215-3693 USA
(617) 747-2146

Visit Berklee Press Online at
www.berkleepress.com

DISTRIBUTED BY

HAL•LEONARD®
CORPORATION
7777 W. BLUEMOUND RD. P.O. BOX 13819
MILWAUKEE, WISCONSIN 53213

Visit Hal Leonard Online at
www.halleonard.com

Contents

PART 1   Melody: Its Components

Part 2   Melody-Harmony Relationships

Preface

intuition and the rational mind in creative writing

The one question my students most often ask me is, "When you compose a song, do you really think of [the technique under discussion]?" I say, "Yes, I do, especially when I get stuck." But then I explain that another more important phenomenon usually occurs while in the throes of writing: because I have absorbed this knowledge, it is available to me at a pace that is faster than thought. I liken the way this happens to learning how to drive a car. In learning to drive, there are so many things to think about at once, it seems nearly impossible to put them all together. Yet driving, after a short time, becomes second nature. We absorb the bit-by-bit information and somehow do what was once thought impossible.

You can't drive by using your rational mind alone; if you tried, you would almost certainly have an accident. Ask yourself, how did you do it? You had to align your mind with your body; after all, your body had practiced moves from accelerator pedal to brakes to signal lights, to looking ahead and behind (through mirrors), to turning the steering wheel in the right direction, and so on. You hadn't stopped using your mind; your mind had simply found its rightful place in the act of driving. When you compose a song, something similar occurs.

Just as in driving, if you only use your rational mind in composing a song, you will most likely have an undesirable result—a dry, unmoving group of notes, logically organized, but emotionally barren. A song that moves others must be written by someone who has been moved, who has felt moments of inspiration, who has had an intuitive experience in the actual process of writing. The contents of this book may seem far removed from the intuitive process. It is full of information that will take time and practice to be absorbed. Once you understand what it offers, allow your mind its rightful place in the art of composing a song.

Intuition in songwriting involves more than your body and mind. It involves your emotions as well. In fact, your emotions and spirit usually are the driving forces in writing a song. If, however, your body and mind are not aligned with your emotional/spiritual self, the intuitive moment may never appear—or if it does, and your body and mind are not prepared to carry out its wishes, that precious moment will be lost (and so will that potentially great song). This book is meant to help you prepare for that moment.

Acknowledgments

Many of the concepts in this book are borrowed from Pat Pattison's work on lyric structure. His enthusiasm for teaching songwriting, along with his personal encouragement of my efforts, eased my task of translating these concepts into musical equivalents. I want to thank Bob Weingart for editing parts of this workbook, for providing me with thought-provoking challenges, suggestions, and many ideas, as well as inventing some of the terms I have adopted. Jimmy Kachulis also made some valuable contributions, especially in the chapter on blues/rock.

Scott McCormick and Sammy Epstein, who are not members of the Songwriting Department but who have a special interest in scholarly endeavors, deserve special praise for editing and contributing many helpful suggestions. I thank my entire faculty for participating in the sometimes arduous task of reading, discussing, and clarifying the language and techniques found within this book. I especially want to thank Ted Pease, distinguished professor, for his support ever since my arrival at Berklee College of Music, and for giving me the chance to write a serious book on a subject not heretofore taken seriously enough by the academic music community.

Introduction

Much of this book is involved in explaining the way music works. I believe that it is important for anyone trying to find his or her personal creative voice to seek out the *bases* of sounds and their organization —sounds such as the major scale or rhythmic patterns that have been retained from nursery rhymes, childrens' songs, and popular songs, old and new. Understanding the materials and building blocks of music opens many doors, doors that remain closed to those who can't get beyond their limited knowledge.

The first part of this book concentrates on melody, a subject not usually taught in depth or even broached in most music colleges because, unlike harmony, no theories of melody have been sufficiently codified to have become a part of academia. The study of melody is the clearest way to present the tonal and rhythmic materials of songwriting.

The second part of the book concentrates on the ways in which melody and harmony interact. There are some additional subjects and vocabulary presented that are so intrinsic to present-day songwriting that to have omitted them would have done you a disservice. Please do not interpret the sequential order of the presentation of the subjects in this book as a step-by-step methodology for composing songs. There are many ways to compose a song, such as beginning with a lyric, a melody, a chord progression, a bass line, a guitar riff, a drum pattern, and so on.

There are no rules in this book. Only tools and techniques are presented. This is the only way I know to help you find both your personal voice and those universals that may make your songs become truly popular songs.

Once you have a grasp of the basic tools and techniques presented in this workbook and in the classroom, you should experience more freedom to express yourself. When you "get stuck," you will have some real knowledge to turn to in order to get "unstuck" and get on with the song.

PART 1

Melody:
Its Components

Chapter 1

Melody: Some Basics

melody
The two basic elements of music that define melody are pitch and rhythm. Melody is a succession of pitches in rhythm. The melody is usually the most memorable aspect of a song, the one the listener remembers and is able to perform.

melodic phrase
A melodic phrase, much like a sentence or clause in verbal language, usually encompasses a complete musical statement. A melodic phrase usually defines itself by resting or holding or coming to some point of resolution (rhythmically and/or tonally) and, especially in vocal music, is directly related to the natural areas to breathe. Short phrases usually group together to form a longer phrase.

In the following example, phrase1 and phrase 2 group together to form a longer phrase; phrase 3 and phrase 4 group together to form a longer phrase.

Ex.1.1

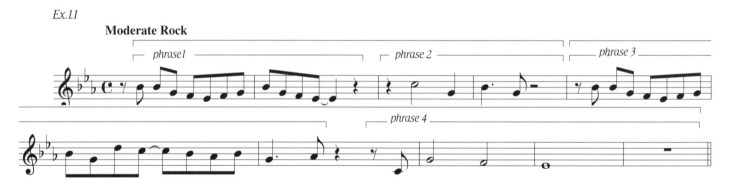

conjunct/disjunct melodic motion
There are two types of melodic motion: conjunct motion, which proceeds by step from one scale degree to the next (i.e., by the interval of a second) and disjunct motion, which proceeds by leap (i.e., by intervals larger than a second).

A melody assumes character by a number of means: its rhythmic structure, its contour, its tonal makeup, and its intervallic content. Most vocal melodies consist of conjunct motion, which is the most natural and comfortable to sing. It is usually the intervallic leaps, however, that give a melody character and cause the melody to assume more of a memorable profile.

Ex.1.2 Conjunct motion produces a smooth vocal line

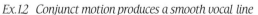

Ex.1.3 Disjunct motion is more difficult to sing.

Ex.1.4 Conjunct and disjunct motion, working together, usually produce a good result.

writing for the voice It is absolutely essential to the craft of songwriting that the writer sing the melody, feel it in the voice, reach for the high notes, and focus on experiencing the relationship between the lyric and the melody. Much of melody writing done for instruments, especially for the piano, is difficult or impossible to sing. The following are to be considered when writing for the voice:

1. How disjunct is the melody? Too many intervallic leaps can cause the melody to be difficult or impossible to sing.

Ex.1.5

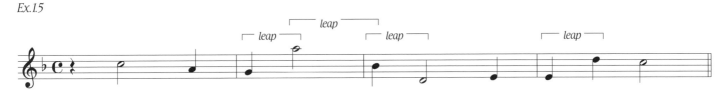

2. Does the vocalist have time to breathe between phrases? Is the phrase so long that it doesn't allow the singer to breathe?

Ex.1.6

3. Is the vocal range of the song too great? Does the range within a section of the song change too quickly?

Ex.1.7

The range of the average pop vocalist is as follows:

Ex.1.8

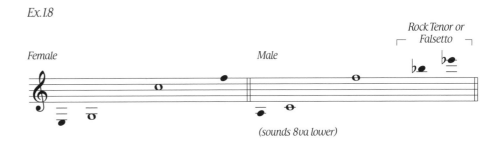

the lead sheet

The lead sheet format reflects the importance of the melody. Harmonic voicings, texture, and orchestration are not found in lead sheets. The lead sheet solely contains the melody, the lyric, and the harmony notated with chord symbols.

guidelines for lead sheet writing

The following guidelines for leadsheet writing are given to help eliminate the usual errors.

1. The melody should be notated in a clear-cut but accurate fashion in the treble clef. Notes and rhythms that are purely embellishments need not appear on the lead sheet.

2. If a section of a song is repeated and some melodic rhythms and pitches are slightly altered (as often happens in verse sections), cue notes should be written for these deviations.

Ex.1.9

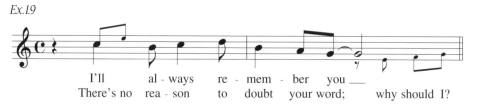

3. Chord symbols should appear directly over the beat or part of the beat on which they are played. It may be necessary to approximate this if a melody note is not sung on the exact rhythm.

Ex.1.10

One of the most common errors is placing a chord in the middle of the bar when the chord is intended to be sounded for the entire measure. This is confusing to a player who must play the chord on the first beat.

Ex.1.11

4. Each syllable of the lyric should be placed directly under the note or notes to which it is sung. Spacing of the music is determined by the length of words and syllables. Improper alignment of lyric to melody is a common mistake that should be avoided, as shown here:

Ex.1.12

Use seven- or eight-stave paper to allow for two or three sets of lyrics to be placed under each stave.

Ex.1.13

An - y - thing's pos - si - ble _____

5. Lyrics may include lowercase and uppercase letters or consist entirely of uppercase letters. Lyrics are always printed.
6. Hyphens are used to separate syllables.

Ex.1.14

Where's he gone? _____ Heav - en. _____

7. "Extended" lines are used for a one-syllable word or for the last syllable of a polysyllabic word that occurs with tied or slurred notes.

Ex.1.15

He'll nev - er, ev - er ___ leave.

8. A slur should be written above or below the note heads for two or more notes assigned to a single syllable.
9. The title should be capitalized and centered on the first page. Indicate "words by" or "lyric by" followed by the lyricist's name and "music by" followed by the composer's name in the upper right section of the first page. It is wise to number the additional pages and to print the song title in the upper right-hand corner of each page.
10. A tempo or groove indication at the upper left of the first page should be included.
11. A copyright notice should be written at the bottom of the first page: Copyright © (year) by (copyright owner).
12. The lead sheet for the song is not an arrangement. In rare cases, however, it may contain music that is not sung, such as an intro- duction/interlude figure that the composer deems intrinsic to the song. The lead sheet may contain a bass figure that is used throughout the song and that is identifiably characteristic of the song. The figure would be written once in the bass clef at the beginning of the lead sheet with an indication to "play through- out song" or "play on every chorus."

Try to keep such indications to an absolute minimum. The lead sheet should represent the most essential ingredients of the song. These ingredients can then be embellished by the vocalist(s), the accompanist, the arranger, or the producer. Do not clutter the lead sheet with arranging ideas or instrumental sections that are optional.

repeat signs Since a lead sheet presents the song in a complete but concise way, the use of first and second endings and other repeat signs should be employed.

Ex.1.16

There is no need to use a repeat sign at the beginning of a piece since the first ending automatically refers back to the beginning. If, however, the repeat does not refer to the beginning of the piece, a repeat sign must be installed at the beginning of the appropriate measure.

Other common and useful repeat signs are as follows:

> **D.C.** (*Da Capo* means "go back to the beginning")
> **D.S.** (*Dal Segno* means "go back to the 𝄋 sign")

In vocal music, it is best to place these signs above the staff and as close to the end of the measure as possible.

Another useful symbol is ⊕, the coda sign. This symbol is used in the last part of a piece where new material has been added to form the ending or the "fade" ending. (Fade endings are often found in recording situations but are seldom used in live performances.)

Often repeat symbols are combined. For example, **D.S. al Coda** means "go to the sign 𝄋, continue until you reach **To Coda** ⊕, and then jump to the place in the manuscript where the coda sign ⊕ appears."

Occasionally a 𝄋𝄋, double sign, is needed. This symbol is only used after the direction D.S. 𝄋 has been used and an additional repeat is necessary.

Written directions such as *"To Next Strain"* or *"Repeat and Fade"* are often used to save space. "To next strain" simply means to go on to the next section of the piece. Some of these shortcuts are somewhat confusing. They should be used only in lead sheets and are not recommended when writing parts for players.

writing tip When actually composing the song, such shortcuts as putting in a repeat sign after four measures in a verse section may discourage creative possibilities and choices that might have existed if you had allowed yourself the space to realize them. (These could be as simple as changing one pitch or rhythm or may entail adding a couple of measures of new music.)

Study the architecture of the sample lead sheet found below, and then read the explanation of the format to confirm that you fully understand the meaning of the repeat symbols and directions.

Ex.1.17

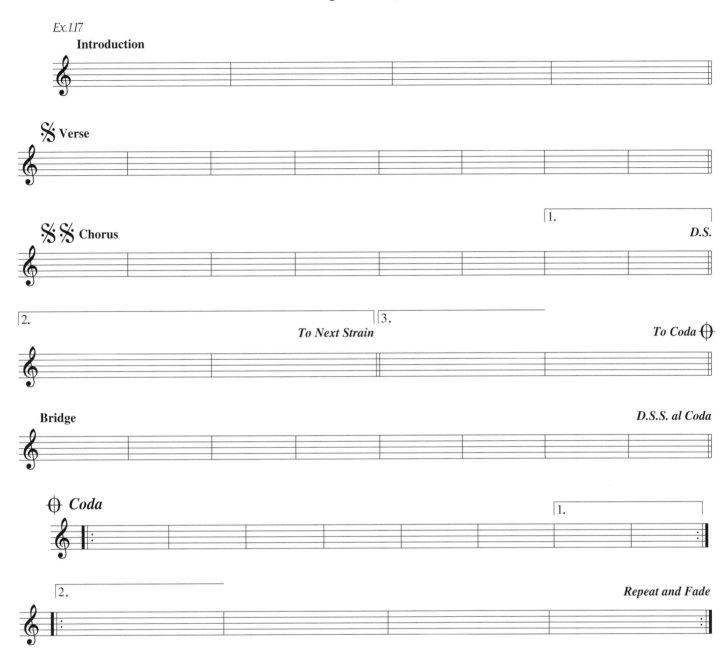

format

Introduction
Verse 1
Chorus (take the 1st ending and D.S.)
Verse 2
Chorus (take 2nd ending, go to the next strain)
Bridge (D.S.S. to the chorus)
Chorus (take 3rd ending and go to the coda)
Coda (take the 1st ending)
Repeat the 2nd ending (four bars) ad infinitum.

Chapter 2

Pitch

Ex. 2.1

Harmonic Number

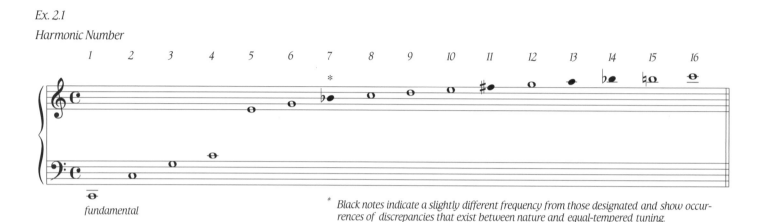

fundamental

* *Black notes indicate a slightly different frequency from those designated and show occurrences of discrepancies that exist between nature and equal-tempered tuning.*

harmonic series The harmonic series is our guide to what is natural and, therefore, is the best place to begin to study tonal music.

Every tone, with the exception of a pure sine wave, is made up of a composite of tones. These tones are called overtones, partials, or harmonics. The strength or amplitude of a partial is usually determined by its placement within the series; the closer to the fundamental, the stronger the partial.

Examine the harmonic series and note the following:

- *The spacing of the series.* The largest intervals are closest to the fundamental; the smallest intervals are farthest from the fundamental.
- *The importance of the perfect 5th.* The placement of the perfect 5th in the series accounts both for its concordance with the fundamental and its strong tendency to move downward to it (as it so often does when it functions as a bass note in a chord progression).
- *The appearance of the major triad within the first five harmonics.* The minor triad built on the fundamental tone does not appear.
- *The strong relationship of the fundamental to the perfect 5th, major 3rd, and minor 7th (not the major 7th!).* The major 7th appears very far from the fundamental in the series.
- *The minor 3rd above the fundamental does not appear in the series.*
- *The subdominant tone (4th degree of the major and minor scales) does not appear in the overtone series.*

the major scale If we now look at the major scale in relation to the overtone series, we have a basis for understanding why some tones tend to need to move or resolve, while other tones tend to remain stationary. All the tones within an overtone series are measured by their relationship to the fundamental; likewise, all the tones within a diatonic system are measured by their relationship to the tonic note. The interesting aspect of our diatonic system, traditional major or minor, is that some of these tones are quite dissonant to the tonic (such as the major 7th and perfect 4th of the major scale), creating a system that has a "built in" kineticism. If we think of the tonic note in a diatonic system as acting like the fundamental of the overtone series, we begin to grasp the discrepancies between the two systems (the former—man-made; the latter—of nature). The various discrepancies between culture and nature within the diatonic system are what create interest and make it a wondrous symbolic reflection of man.

Ex. 2.2

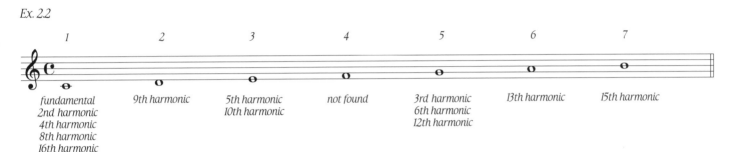

stable and unstable tones All tonal systems are built in a hierarchical structure. There is always one tone, the tonic, which is the most stable. Other tones having a good relationship to the tonic are also labeled "stable." The most stable tones are 1, 3, and 5; 1 is more stable than 5, and 5 is more stable than 3. Other tones that have a more distant relationship to the tonic are labeled "unstable."

Ex. 2.3 Degrees of Stability in Major

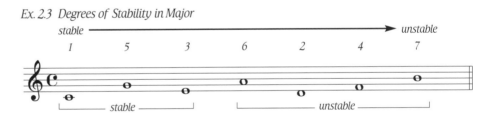

Notice that the most unstable tones in the major scale, 4 and 7, have a half-step relationship to other stable diatonic tones.

tone tendencies We define *stable tones* (st) as 1, 3, 5 of the tonality. *Unstable tones* (ust), since they "need" to move, have intrinsic melodic energy. Unstable tones tend to resolve in a *downward* direction to stable tones. Therefore, 2 resolves to 1; 4 resolves to 3; 6 resolves to 5; 7, because it is most unstable and is one half-step away from the tonic, resolves *upward* to the tonic. These are the "natural" resolutions for the unstable diatonic tones in major.

Ex. 2.4

All chromatic tones are unstable and tend to resolve to the nearest diatonic tone.

Ex. 2.5

b2–1   #1–2   b3–2   #2–3   b5–4   #4–5   b6–5   #5–6   b7–6   #6–7

tonally open and closed phrases

Melodic phrases that end on a stable tone are tonally "closed"; but here, too, are degrees of closure, with the tonic providing the greatest degree of closure. (Think of the final melody note to your favorite song and, chances are, it is the tonic.) Melodic phrases that end on an unstable tone are "open," with the greatest degree of openess provided by 7, the leading tone.

exercise

Establish a major key at the keyboard. Play the tonic note in the bass. Sing the 2nd degree; resolve it to 1. Continue to play the tonic note in the bass. Sing the 3rd degree. Notice that there is less of a need to resolve it—although stable, tones 3 and 5 will only be fully resolved if they move to 1. Now sing the 4th degree; resolve it. Continue this exercise throughout the scale.

independent melody

The purpose of this chapter and other chapters in Part I of this book is to teach you how to create an independent melody, a melody that has enough tonal and rhythmic interest to be satisfying without the necessity of a chordal accompaniment. Measuring the amount of tension or instability in the melody by referring to the tonic note—not to any other harmony—allows you to accomplish this.

In actual melodies, unstable tones do not always resolve to their natural resolutions nor do they necessarily resolve to stable tones at all. We control our melodies by knowing the natural resolution of tones and then choosing to resolve them or not, according to the possible consequences. The consequence of our choices either satisfy expectations, increase expectations, or frustrate expectations.

In Ex. 2.6a, when 6 moves to 7, we have two unstable tones in a row, increasing our expectation; when 7 leaps upward to 2, we have a further increase in melodic tension; when 2 resolves to 1, its natural resolution, it tonally closes the melodic phrase.

Ex. 2.6a

6   7   2   1

In Ex. 2.6b, our intention is to have not quite as obvious and closed a resolution. In this case, 2 resolves to 3. The consequence of our choice is a tonal closure that is not completely at rest.

Ex. 2.6b

Because they need to resolve, *unstable tones* (ust) create expectations. The movement of a point of tension (for example, an unstable tone) to a goal area that provides release (for example, a stable tone) creates forward motion. *Stable tones* (st) are often employed at cadences when termination or resolution is desired. Examine the ending notes of each of the following phrases. Note the increase in forward motion created by unstable tones appearing at the end of phrases.*

Ex. 2.7

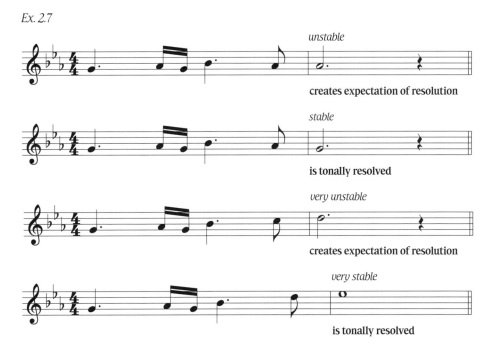

The following melody, derived from the previous example, demonstrates that even if the rhythm of the phrase and most of the pitches of the melody remain the same in successive phrases, interest can be achieved by the conscious use of tone tendencies and stable-to-unstable relationships at the endings of phrases.

Ex. 2.8

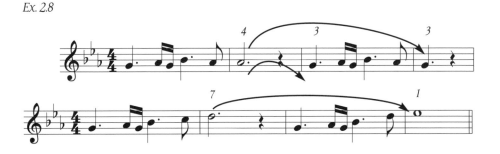

---

* *Before playing or singing this example or any of the purely melodic examples, first establish the key by playing and singing the scale of the key of the example. Then play and hold the tonic note in the bass, and try to be aware of the tonal implications of each melody note as it sounds against it.*

Both the *last* note of the phrase and the *first* note of the phrase are important focal areas. It is possible to make a smooth connection from one phrase to another by making the first note of the second phrase the resolution of the last note of the previous phrase.

One can create forward motion in a melody by using strategically placed unstable tones to create expectations. In the following melody, unstable tones create expectations at the end of phrases; stable tones, occurring either at the beginnings or endings of phrases, satisfy those expectations by resolving them.

Ex. 2.9

unstable tones ending phrases An unstable tone that ends a phrase calls attention to itself and to the expected tone of resolution. Many folk and traditional songs provide us with excellent examples of this type of activity. Each of the following two examples have phrase structures that sectionalize the music into two mirror parts and that draw attention to the tension/release factor at work as each section ends.

Ex. 2.10

My Old Kentucky Home

Stephen Foster

Ex. 2.11

Yellow Rose of Texas

Traditional

writing tip Before beginning to compose, establish the key by playing and singing the scale of the key in which you wish to compose. Then play and hold the tonic note in the bass and try to be aware of the tonal implications of each melody note as it sounds against it.

assignment *Write a diatonic melody in a major key that contains four two-measure phrases. (See example of finished assignment.)*

- *The first phrase must begin on a stable tone and end on an unstable tone.*
- *The second phrase must begin on an unstable tone and end on a stable tone that resolves the last note of the first phrase.*
- *The third phrase must begin on an unstable tone and end on an unstable tone.*
- *The fourth phrase may begin on either a stable or an unstable tone. It must end on a stable tone that resolves the last note of the third phrase.*

Ex. 2.12 Example of finished assignment

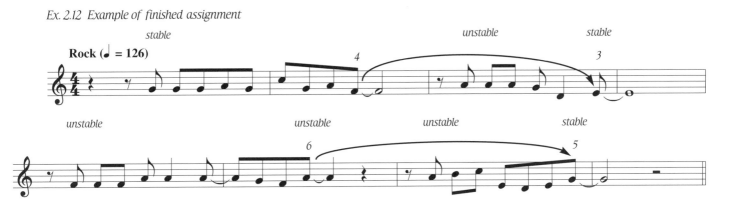

Chapter 3

Rhythm

pulse, meter, and rhythm
Music takes place in time. It is in the control of time that a player and/or composer prove their mettle. Musical time is measured by pulses or beats, meter, and rhythm.

Pulse is a series of undifferentiated even beats. All pulses in a series are by definition exactly alike.

Ex. 3.1

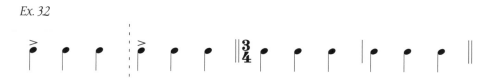

Meter is a measurement of the number of pulses between regularly recurring accents. Meter is the grouping of pulses.

Ex. 3.2

Music that tends to emphasize body movements, such as marching and dancing, has a more pronounced meter stated or strongly implied.

Ex. 3.3

Music that is contemplative, such as Gregorian chant, tends to de-emphasize the meter or not have meter.

Ex. 3.4

Rhythm is ever changing but can be measured by its relationship to the meter.

Ex. 3.5

Rhythm is our most basic and important structural element. At a micro level, it controls the inner structure of each phrase and relationships between individual phrases. At a macro level, it controls the form of the entire musical composition.

In order to show you the importance of rhythm, I'll draw an analogy between rhythm and the body. Rhythm is the skeleton, controlling the basic shape; pitch is the muscle and flesh; arrangement and orchestration provide the clothes, makeup, and accessories. Without the skeleton, everything else collapses, yet few people notice or even think about it!

stress symbols The notation of rhythm can be transcribed into stress symbols used in poetic scansion: / Primary Stress, // Secondary Stress, — Unstressed. Stress symbols demonstrate strong/weak relationships between rhythms that are not apparent with music notation.

Any group of two evenly divided rhythms forms a stress pattern of Strong / Weak —.

Ex. 3.6a Metric Stress

Ex. 3.6b Rhythmic Stress

Any group of four evenly divided rhythms form a stress pattern of Strong /, Weak —, Moderately Strong //, Weak —.

Ex. 3.7a Metric Stress

Ex. 3.7b Rhythmic Stress

Any group of three evenly divided rhythms form a stress pattern of
Strong /, Weak —, Weak —.

Ex. 3.8a Metric Stress

Ex. 3.8b Rhythmic Stress

summative stress The stress pattern of a given rhythm reflects the concurrent metric
stress and rhythmic stress. It also reflects the divisional or subdivisional
stress pattern that has occurred in the rhythms of the previous beat. The
combined result is called the *summative stress.*

Ex. 3.9 Given Rhythm

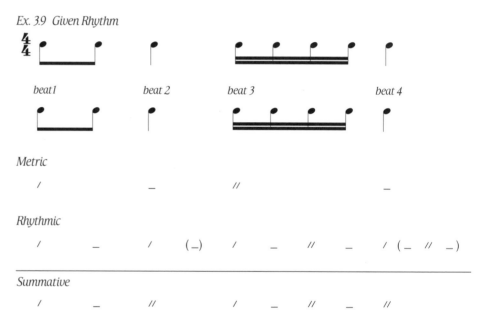

Metric stress always has a summative effect on whatever level of division or subdivision of the beat is taking place.

In compound meters or in duple meters containing triplet rhythms,
the stress patterns work summatively with each other.

Ex. 3.10 Metric Stress

Divisional or Subdivisional Stress

Summational Stress

additional considerations in stress

Syncopation, the accenting of a normally weak beat or part of a beat, causes the syncopated note(s) to be more heavily stressed.

Ex. 3.11

Anticipations receive the stress of the beat anticipated and an additional stress due to the syncopation.

Ex. 3.12

A note following a rest receives more emphasis (unless it is less than the value of the note that it follows, in which case it is simply acting as a pickup to the following beat). See beat 2 in the examples below.

Ex. 3.13a Note sounding on the first beat

Ex. 3.13b Rest on the first beat

The most important factor in determining how much stress a note receives is the relationship of its rhythm to the meter and to the rhythmic divisions or subdivisions taking place within the meter. Other factors contributing to how much stress a note receives are 1) duration, 2) pitch, 3) accent and 4) dynamic level.

Ex. 3.14a Duration

Ex. 3.14b Pitch (compare a to b)

Ex. 3.14c Accent (including syncopation and anticipation)

Ex. 3.14d Dynamics

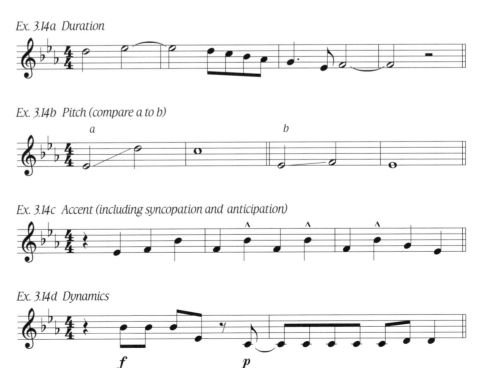

It is difficult to notate with complete accuracy the myriad degrees of stress within an ever-changing rhythmic setting. The best we can do is use the stress symbols available to show the relative strength or weakness of any given rhythm.

Study the following rhythms and their corresponding stress analysis.

Ex. 3.16a

Ex. 3.16b

Ex. 3.16c

Ex. 3.16d

Ex. 3.16e

Ex. 3.16f

Ex. 3.16g
Shuffle

assignment *Indicate stress notation for each of the following rhythms.*

Ex. 3.17

1.

2.

3.

4.

5.

6.

7.

8.

Shuffle

9.

One of the compositional variables discussed in Pat Pattison's book *Managing Lyric Structure* (Berklee Press, HL50481582) is the *rhythm of the phrase.* Music notation allows us to have much more control of this variable. It allows us to control the exact placement and duration of strong and weak stresses within the meter. A pattern like / — / — / can be expressed in music in many ways.

Ex. 3.18

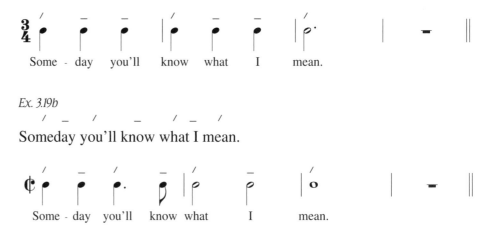

Understanding how lyric stress works with music notation provides many options when you attempt to set a lyric. Study the following lyric: "Someday you'll know what I mean."

Ex. 3.19a

Someday you'll know what I mean.

Some - day you'll know what I mean.

Ex. 3.19b

Someday you'll know what I mean.

Some - day you'll know what I mean.

The stress notation for the phrase can be expressed:

Ex. 3.20

Someday you'll know what I mean.

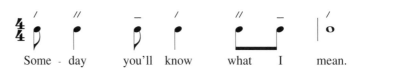

Some - day you'll know what I mean.

Once you choose to set the lyric in exact rhythm (which music notation provides), there should be little doubt by your listener as to what is being emphasized in the lyric.

This same stress pattern may be expressed musically in other rhythms and in other meters, for example:

Ex. 3.21a

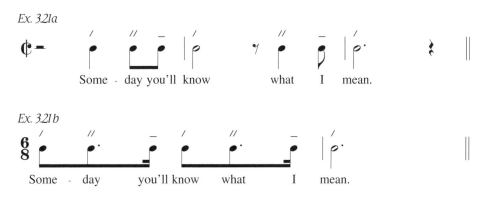

Some - day you'll know   what   I   mean.

Ex. 3.21b

Some - day   you'll know   what   I   mean.

masculine/feminine endings

The terms "masculine" and "feminine" are used in analysis of poetry and lyrics. A word ending on an accented syllable is said to have a *masculine* ending; one ending on an unaccented syllable, a *feminine* ending. "Believe" ends on an accented syllable and if used as the last line of a lyric, it would yield a masculine ending.

Ex. 3.22a

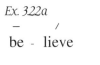

be - lieve

I've   tried   to   be - lieve

If this phrase were to read "I've tried to believe you," it would yield a feminine ending.

Ex. 3.22b

be - lieve you

I've   tried   to   be - lieve   you

Another important consideration is words that end on a secondary stress, words such as "melody" or "beautiful." Placing the last syllable of either of these words on the first beat of a measure would cause a problem in prosody, i.e., the matching of musical accent to word or syllabic accent.

Ex. 2.23

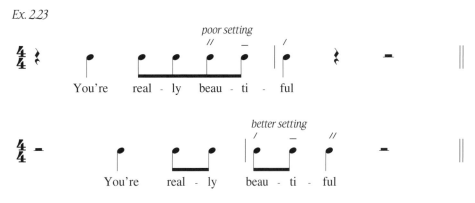

poor setting

You're   real - ly   beau - ti - ful

better setting

You're   real - ly   beau - ti - ful

beyond simple prosody There are many possible musical settings for any given lyric. Choosing the one that really works is not simply a matter of adjusting the rhythm to yield the correct accenting of syllables. Also to be considered are the exact placement of the lyric within the measure, how much space is needed between phrases, the prolongation and accenting of certain words you feel need to be emphasized, the choice of melodic pitch and harmonies that help color the entire phrase and so on. All of these and more go into the setting of a lyric in order to achieve the subtle emotional shadings to be expressed.

exercise *Study the lyric of the first verse and chorus of "Love Is You."*

Love Is You

Lyric by Denise Utt

A rainy day

But that's O.K.

I'll listen to my music

And I'll drift away.

Inside of me

I've got a song

It's been playin'

Ever since you turned it on.

Love is new

Love is free

No one's given more

Than what you've given me.

Love is good

Love is true

I've searched the whole world over

And I've found

Love is you.

Try to set the lyric using only rhythm. After you have finished, compare what you have done to the actual setting of the song. (See Ex. 9.8)

writing tip This exercise is a fine one to do with songs you have not heard before. Most recordings come with notated lyrics. When you purchase a recording or borrow one from a friend or the library, choose not to listen to the recording until after doing this exercise. Instead, read the lyrics and choose one that attracts you, and then attempt to set it. (You may even choose to create an entire musical setting instead of only using rhythm.) Finally, compare your setting with the way the lyrics were set by the writers for the recording. By the way, this exercise may reward you with very usable music; in doing this project, you will have borrowed only the form and rhythmic structure of the lyric. The music you will have created will be yours to use with a different lyric!

assignment *Place stress symbols over the syllables in each of the following lyrics. Then, adhering to your choice of stress, place each of the lyrics in two different, yet valid, rhythmic settings.*

1. Over and over and over again

2. It's too late to turn back now

3. Remember me,

   And I promise I'll remember you.

Chapter 4

Tone Tendencies

**immediate resolution,
delayed resolution,
and no resolution**

An unstable tone (circled in the examples) may resolve immediately,

Ex. 4.1

or resolve after a number of beats,

Ex. 4.2

or even after a number of measures,

Ex. 4.3

or not resolve at all.

Ex. 4.4

See "The Long and Winding Road" (Ex 19.4) for an excellent example of a delayed resolution.

The significance of the stability/instability relationship of tones is affected by the rhythmic placement of those tones within the measure and within the phrase. Tones found at the beginning of a phrase (unless the notes are simply pickups) and the ending note of a phrase are especially important in determining its tonal design.*

Examine the following melody and attempt to designate the important tonal movements taking place within it.

Ex. 4.5

---

* *This subject is more fully covered in Chapter 7, under the heading of Melodic Outline.*

The tonal nature of the entire phrase should be examined. Ask yourself the following: Does the phrase begin in a stable area and cadence in an unstable one or vice versa? Does the phrase remain unstable or stable throughout?

The first phrase in the example moves from a stable area (the pickup notes have little significance except to focus attention on the downbeat G, which is stable) to A♭, an unstable tone. The second phrase moves from D, an unstable tone, to G, a stable tone that resolves the A♭ that had ended the first phrase. The third phrase begins (again, disregarding the pickup notes) on an unstable tone and remains unstable.

Ex. 4.6

assignment
(see ex. 4.6)

1. *Circle all unstable tones.*
2. *Study each phrase, noticing the tones that receive more stress within each measure.*
3. *Designate a significant immediate resolution by drawing an arrow above the staff from the circled unstable tone to the stable tone of resolution.*
4. *Designate a significant delayed resolution by drawing an arrow below the staff from the circled unstable tone to the stable tone of resolution.*
5. *Draw an asterisk above significant tones that have no resolution.*
6. *Designate the tonal movements taking place within the phrase by designating stable or unstable above the staff at the beginning, middle (if significant), and end of each phrase.*

Ex. 4.7

Moderate rock

3.

Slowly

4.

Rock ballad

5.

Moderately fast

6.

Moderately

7.

Chapter 5

Symmetry/Asymmetry

compositional variables A number of compositional variables are involved in discerning whether you've created a symmetric or asymmetric section of music:

1. the number of phrases
2. the length of the phrases (how many measures in each phrase)
3. the rhythm of phrases
4. the order of the phrases

the number of phrases An even number of phrases *of the same length* will produce a balanced section of music. An odd number of phrases of the same length will produce an unbalanced section of music.

For example, two two-measure phrases will produce a balanced structure,

Ex. 5.1

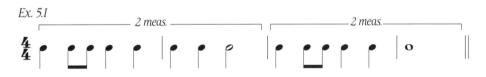

whereas three two-measure phrases will produce an unbalanced structure.

Ex. 5.2

Three one-measure phrases (an odd number of phrases of the same length) are unbalanced.

Ex. 5.3

However, three one-measure phrases would be balanced by an additional group of three one-measure phrases (two groups of three phrases).

Ex. 5.4

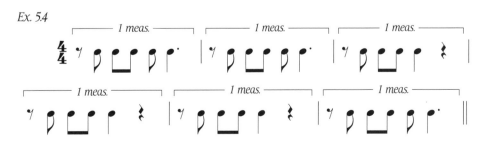

You may ask if the three one-measure phrases could be balanced by one one-measure phrase and one two-measure phrase. The answer is yes, they could; to be more exact, the number of measures would balance each other, but the number of phrases would not balance each other. The number of phrases (in the case cited, three phrases answered by two phrases) would affect the structure and cause it to be less balanced. Your question anticipates the next compositional variable—the length of the phrases.

balance vs. symmetry You've also probably been wondering why I've used the term "balance" instead of "symmetry" in the previous examples. I use the term "balance" as a catchall that includes varying degrees of balance; a section can be *more* balanced or *less* balanced. I reserve the term "symmetric" for use only when all of the compositional variables are balanced.

Before we move on to the next variable, it's probably wise to ask if complete balance or symmetry is something composers strive for. The answer is, generally, no! Symmetry in all art forms tends to be boring, whereas balance is usually a sought-after ideal. Another way to think of symmetry is that it is an absolute by which to measure the degrees of balance or imbalance in any section of music.

Study the two illustrations. The first is symmetric; the second is not, but it is balanced. Which one holds more interest?

Ex. 5.5

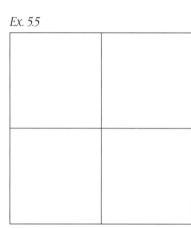 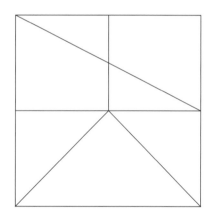

phrase lengths; phrasal balance We can view song structure at a macro level, for example, how one section of a song balances another, or at a micro level, for example, how one phrase balances another.

Phrasal balance is analyzed by the phrase length. It is determined by comparing the number of measures in one phrase to the number of measures in the following phrase or phrases.

A phrase followed by another phrase with the same number of measures, such as a two-measure phrase followed by another two-measure phrase, produces a *balanced* phrase structure.

Ex. 5.6

A phrase followed by two or more phrases that equal its length produces a *balanced* phrase structure, such as a four-measure phrase followed by two two-measure phrases producing a balanced phrase structure.

Ex. 5.7

A phrase followed by another phrase of a different length, such as a two-measure phrase followed by a one-measure phrase, produces an *unbalanced* phrase structure.

Ex. 5.8

exercise *1. Create a second phrase that does not balance the first one.*

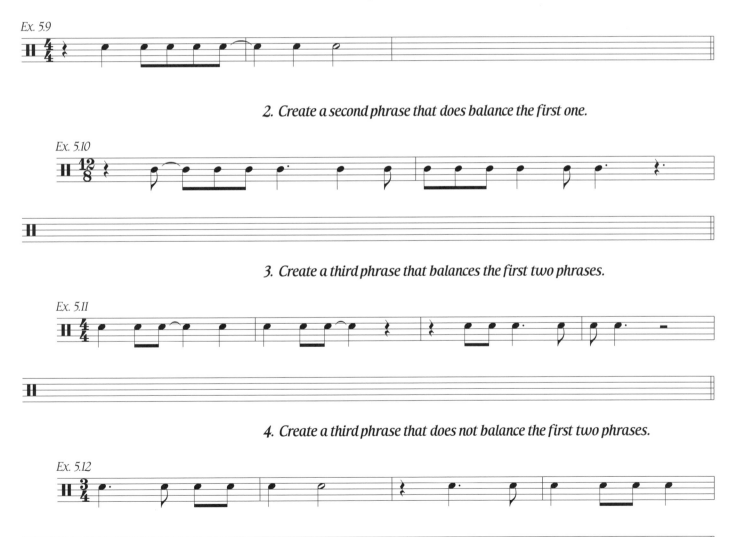

2. Create a second phrase that does balance the first one.

3. Create a third phrase that balances the first two phrases.

4. Create a third phrase that does not balance the first two phrases.

the rhythm of the phrase

The rhythms within the phrases must be considered when analyzing phrasal symmetry/asymmetry. Upon examining the following example, we realize that although balance at the phrasal/metric level has been achieved, the rhythms of the second two measures do not correspond or "match" the rhythms of the first two measures. The rhythms are *asymmetric.*

Ex. 5.13

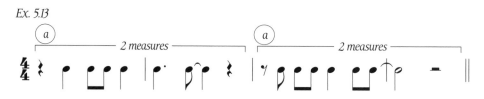

The above example provides us with a common event in music: the simultaneous occurrence of both balance (at the metric level), and asymmetry (at the rhythmic level). In order for the above example to be made completely symmetric, we would have to either:

1. Rewrite the second phrase to match the first phrase.

Ex. 5.14a

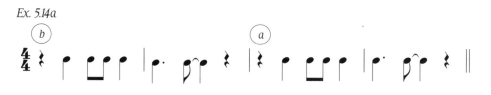

2. Rewrite the first phrase to match the second phrase.

Ex. 5.14b

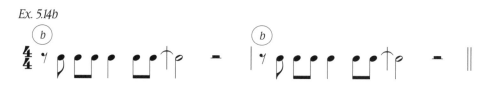

3. Create four more measures with the same rhythmic structure to match our first four measures.

Ex. 5.14c

matched, inexactly matched, and unmatched phrases

A *matched phrase* must be the same phrase length as the first phrase, and its last rhythm(s) (i.e., corresponding to a poetic foot: e.g., Iamb - /, Trochee /-, Spondee / /) must be articulated on the same beat or same part of the beat as the last articulated rhythm of the first phrase.

Ex. 5.15a Matched Phrase

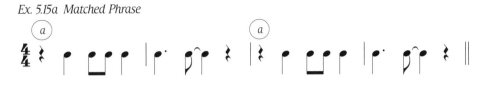

The term "last articulated rhythm" needs clarification. If a note is tied, the second note is not articulated; a slur that may involve two or more notes sung to the same syllable acts exactly the same way as a tie in that only the first note is articulated—all the rest are carried in the same breath.

Ex. 5.15b

Now life is so aim - less _   Not feel-ing so blame - less _

If the second phrase is the same phrase length as the first phrase, but some of its rhythm is different—yet its last rhythm is articulated on the same beat or same part of the beat as the last articulated rhythm of the first phrase—it is called an *inexactly matched phrase.*

Ex. 5.16 Inexactly Matched Phrase

The terms *matched phrase* and *inexactly matched phrase* both refer to two compositional variables: the length of the phrases as well as the rhythm of the phrases (specifically, the ending rhythm).

If a second phrase is the same phrase length as the first phrase, but its last rhythm is not articulated on the same beat or same part of the beat as the last articulated rhythm of the first phrase, it is *unmatched.*

Ex. 5.17 Unmatched Phrase

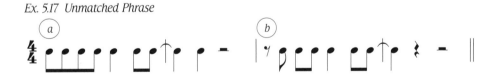

A second phrase that has a different phrase length from the first phrase is also considered an *unmatched phrase.*

Ex. 5.18

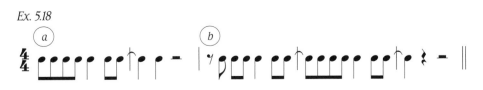

assignment *Create a second phrase. The rhythms of the second phrase will either be matched (a), inexactly matched (a') or unmatched (b). Label each phrase with a letter. (See Ex. 5.19)*

Ex. 5.19 Examples of Finished Assignment

1. Matched

2. Inexactly Matched

3. Unmatched

Ex. 5.20

1. Matched

2. Inexactly Matched

3. Unmatched

4. Unmatched

5. Matched

6. Unmatched

7. Inexactly Matched

assignment *Create four original phrases and then create a second phrase to each as designated.*

Ex. 5.21

correspondence of matched phrases with rhyme Recognizing matched (or inexactly matched) phrases helps a songwriter find areas where rhyme can be used most effectively.

Ex. 5.22

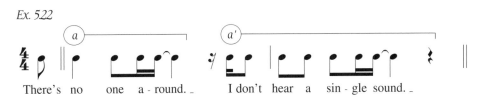

Of course, not every matched phrase need produce a corresponding rhyme. This might cause the song to be too predictable.

outer matching Quite often, a long phrase is followed by two shorter phrases that together equal its phrase length or, conversely, two short phrases are followed by a phrase that equals their combined lengths. If the phrase ending such a section of music is in a balancing position and its rhythms match the rhythms at the end of the phrase or phrases it is balancing, it is called *outer matching. Outer matching* is designated by a letter naming the new phrase followed by a hyphen and letter designating the phrase that is matched. In the following example, the (c) indicates that it is a different phrase length from either (a) or (b) ; the (c-b) indicates that the ending of the (c) phrase and the (b) phrase are rhythmically matched; and that the total number of measures in (c) balances (a) + (b) .

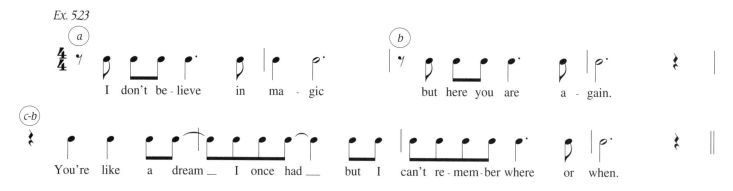

Ex. 5.23

(a) I don't be-lieve in ma - gic

(b) but here you are a - gain.

(c-b) You're like a dream __ I once had __ but I can't re - mem-ber where or when.

matched rhythms

If a rhythm in a phrase is repeated or if a rhythm in one phrase is used in a second phrase (whether or not the second phrase is of the same length), it is referred to as a *matched rhythm*.

Ex. 5.24

Frequently, phrases of unequal length are given ending rhythms that match one another. In those cases, the term *outer rhythmic matching* may be used.

Ex. 5.25

(a) (b)

inner rhythmic matching

A second phrase may contain an internal rhythm pattern that matches and occurs in a parallel position to an internal rhythm pattern appearing in the first phrase. The name given to this occurrence is *inner rhythmic matching*. Inner rhythmic matching corresponds to areas in the lyric where an inner rhyme may be employed quite effectively.

Ex. 5.26

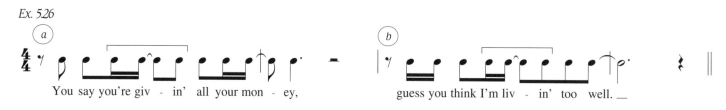

(a) You say you're giv - in' all your mon - ey,

(b) guess you think I'm liv - in' too well. __

Notice that the phrases are not matched; just a rhythm within the phrases is matched. Inner rhythmic matching refers to internal rhythm matching whether or not the total rhythm of the phrases are matched.

Your ability to perceive matched phrases and matched rhythms, including inner matchings and outer matchings, increases your ability to make informed choices, especially concerning rhymes. If a phrase matches, it invites a rhyme. You then must decide whether you feel a rhyme is necessary, desirable, or appropriate at that given point in the song.

open and closed   The terms *open* and *closed* are general terms that can be applied to each of the elements of a song. These terms are especially useful when examining cadential areas where there is some pause or indication of musical punctuation. The element of pitch is very powerful in determining whether a cadential area is open or closed. Stable tones are more likely to sound closed at a cadence than unstable tones. The most stable tone—the tonic of the key—provides the greatest amount of closure. If you have any doubts concerning this, just think of the ending melody note of any song you know; you'll probably hear the tonic.

Any symmetric phrase stucture will provide closure, e.g., look at the following.

Ex. 5.27

When we combine the element of pitch with the above rhythms, the question of whether the section is open or closed may become difficult to answer. In the example below, the phrase structure is closed; the pitch is open because the last pitch, "D," is unstable in the key of C. The total effect is open or, at least, somewhat open. Obviously, the element of pitch is a very powerful one.

Ex. 5.28

If I were to continue to compose this piece, keeping the same rhythms and phrase structure, it would be possible to complete the section by ending on a stable pitch, thereby completely closing both elements.

Ex. 5.29

exercise *Are the following sections open or closed? If open, what compositional variables make the section open: rhythm, pitch or both? If closed, what compositional variables are giving the section a sense of closure: rhythm, pitch, or both?*

Ex. 5.30

assignment

1. *Create an eight-measure section of music that both tonally and rhythmically closes.*

2. *Create an eight-measure section of music that rhythmically closes but remains tonally open.*

36

Chapter 6

Melody in Minor

overtone series   When we examine the tones of the overtone series, we cannot locate the minor third above the fundamental. This has always been a problem for music theorists, especially since music of nearly every culture has incorporated minor into its musical vocabulary. Minor presents a symbolic polarity to major and has come to represent sadness, darkness, and instability, as opposed to major's happiness, lightness, and stability. Since music is an abstract art, these connotations are all suspect. They do hint, however, at the acoustic discrepancy that is intrinsic to the very nature of minor.

Ex. 6.1 Overtone Series (based on the fundamental G)

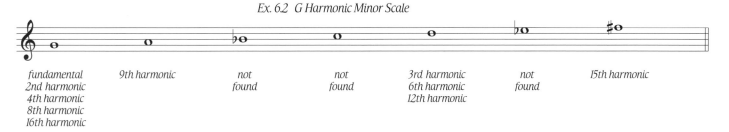

fundamental

* *Black notes indicate a slightly different frequency from those designated and show occurrences of discrepancies that exist between nature and equal-tempered tuning.*

Ex. 6.2 G Harmonic Minor Scale

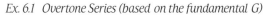

fundamental	9th harmonic	not	not	3rd harmonic	not	15th harmonic
2nd harmonic		found	found	6th harmonic	found	
4th harmonic				12th harmonic		
8th harmonic						
16th harmonic						

the minor scales   The three forms of minor scales presented below are the most commonly used.

Ex. 6.3 Natural Minor or Aeolian

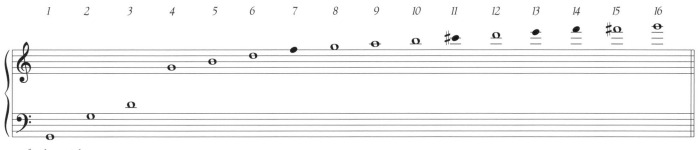

Ex. 6.4 Harmonic Minor

Ex. 6.5 Melodic Minor

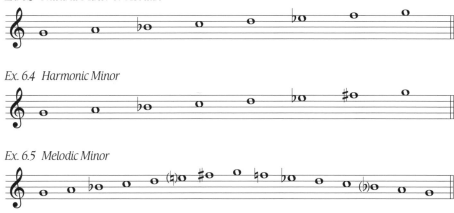

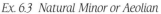

The *tone tendencies* for the first five scale degrees in each of the above scales are the same.

Ex. 6.6

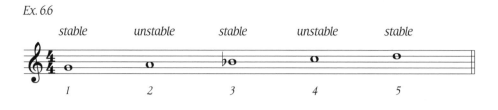

The tone tendencies of most of the members of this group are similar to the tone tendencies found in major. The stable tones are 1, ♭3, and 5.

The tendency is for 2 to resolve to 1. However, 2, because of its half-step relationship to ♭3, may rise quite naturally to it: ♭3 is a stable tone! The tendency is for 4 to resolve to ♭3 and, of course, 5 is stable. The differences in these three forms of minor scales exist in the 6th and 7th degrees.

natural minor or Aeolian mode The natural minor scale or Aeolian mode contains a ♭6, which has a strong tendency to resolve to 5. The ♭7 has a tendency to resolve to 1 but is much more neutral than 7, which has a much stronger pull toward 1 (hence the term "leading tone"). Remember that ♭7 is the 7th partial in the overtone series and, though considered an "unstable tone," is considerably more stable than the major 7th. The lack of a leading tone gives a characteristic placid quality to this scale.

Ex. 6.7

harmonic minor The harmonic minor scale can be built from the natural minor scale by raising the 7th degree one half-step (hence, supplying the leading tone).

The harmonic minor scale contains ♭6 (which has a strong tendency to resolve to 5) but also contains the leading tone with its strong tendency to resolve to 1.

Ex. 6.8

The very unstable ♭6 and raised 7 cause the harmonic minor scale to cadence much more forcibly than the placid natural minor. The melodic movement from ♭6 to 7 or 7 to ♭6 is a rather uncomfortable one in that the strong tendencies of these scale degrees are ignored and are replaced by the interval of an augmented 2nd, a rather awkward interval.

Ex. 6.9

melodic minor   The melodic minor scale can be built from the natural minor scale by raising the 6th and 7th degrees one half-step in its ascending form and lowering the 6th and 7th degrees (restoring the natural minor scale) in its descending form.

  The 6th and 7th degrees in the ascending form are the same as in major and have the same tone tendencies found in major. The ascending movement from raised 6 to raised 7 is much more flowing (or melodic) than is the ♭6 to raised 7 movement found in the harmonic minor scale. The descending form uses the neutral quality of the ♭7 to move to ♭6 instead of employing 7, which has a strong tendency to resolve to 1.

assignment   *1. Write a melody in natural minor that uses a phrase structure consisting of* Ⓐ *(two measures)* Ⓑ *(two measures)* Ⓒ *(four measures).*
2. Write a melody in melodic minor (using ascending and descending forms) that has a phrase structure consisting of Ⓐ *(two measures)* Ⓐ *(two measures* Ⓐ *(two measures)* Ⓑ *(two measures). (See Ex. 6.11.)*

Ex. 6.11 Example of finished assignment

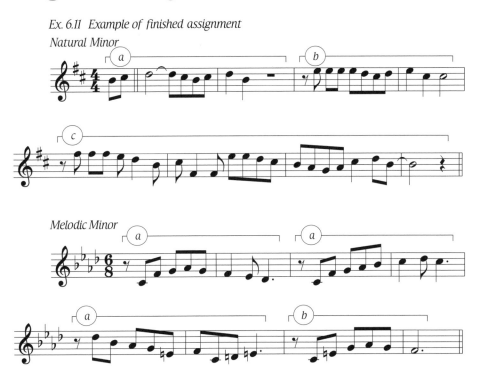

Chapter 7

Melodic Outline; Melodic Contour

melodic outline   The most important notes of a melody, referred to as "structural tones," form its melodic outline. These tones are usually found:

1. On strong beats of a measure, for instance, in 4/4 on beats 1 and 3.
2. On notes that have longer time values in comparison to notes that surround them or on repeated notes that have a combined longer time value in comparison to notes that surround them.
3. On accented notes or pronounced syncopations and anticipations.
4. On the beginning note of a phrase. (This is usually the first down-beat if the phrase begins on a pickup.)
5. On the ending note of a phrase.
6. On the highest or lowest notes of a phrase.

The ability to designate the outline of a melody allows you to control your melody's contour. You may then choose notes that embellish it in interesting, musically satisfying ways.

The melodic outline is given directly above the melody:

Ex. 7.1 Melodic Outline

Many novice songwriters are not aware of the importance of creating a strong melodic outline and write melodies that go "nowhere" as in the following example:

Ex. 7.2

Melodic Outline

melodic step progression   The most comfortable way for a melody to move is by conjunct motion. This applies not only to note-to-note melodic movement but also to large-scale motion between notes of the melodic outline.

Ex. 7.3 Step Progression

embellishing the melodic outline   A number of devices can be used to embellish or connect the structural tones.

Ex. 7.4 Melodic Outline

1. Repeated Tones—repeat the tone rhythmically.

Ex. 7.5

2. Neighbor Tones—use a neighbor tone pattern. *A neighbor tone* is an embellishing tone that occurs stepwise between a structural tone and its repetition. When it appears above the structural tone, it is called an *upper neighbor (UN)*. When it appears below the structural tone, it is called a *lower neighbor (LN)* to the structural tone.

   A neighbor tone is usually of shorter rhythmic value than the structural tone. Though it can appear on or off the beat, it is more usual for it to appear off the beat.

Ex. 7.6

3. Changing Tones—use a changing tone pattern. A *changing tone (CT)* is a two-note embellishing figure using both the upper neighbor and the lower neighbor tones of a structural tone.

Ex. 7.7

4. Scalar Patterns—use a scalar pattern. *A scalar pattern (SC)* links two or more structural tones more than a second apart through stepwise motion. The scalar tones are usually of shorter rhythmic value than the structural tones. Though they can appear on or off the beat, it is more usual for them to appear off the beat.

Ex. 7.8a

   Included in this category is the *passing tone (PT)*, which links two structural tones a 3rd apart through stepwise motion. If the two structural tones are more than a 3rd apart, the term "scalar pattern" is used.

Ex. 7.8b

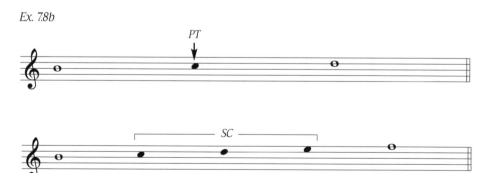

5. Anticipation—use an anticipation. An *anticipation (Ant)* is the same tone as the structural tone it anticipates. It is usually of shorter rhythmic value than the structural tone and usually appears on a weak beat or on the weak part of the beat. (The use of the term anticipation does not refer here to a tied rhythmic anticipation but instead refers to a pitch that is articulated twice, once before the structural tone and again as the structural tone.)

Ex. 7.9

6. Leap—leap (L) from one structural tone to the next structural tone. If two structural tones are more than a second apart, you may choose to connect them using a scalar pattern or simply leap from one structural tone to the next.

Ex. 7.10

Leap from one structural tone to a note of shorter value. Leap from it to the next structural tone. Since no harmony is being stated, your choice of notes is less limited.

Ex. 7.11

7. Combine embellishing devices—be adventuresome! Use combinations of all the embellishing and connecting devices, but don't ever lose track of the structural tones.

Ex. 7.12

analysis of structural tones and embellishing tones

All structural tones have diamond noteheads. Embellishing tones are labeled as follows:

SC = Scalar pattern. Use brackets to designate the scalar pattern.
PT = Passing tone
UN = Upper neighbor tone
LN = Lower neighbor tone
CT = Changing tone pattern
Ant = Anticipation
➞ L = Leapt to
L ➞ = Leapt from

Ex. 7.13

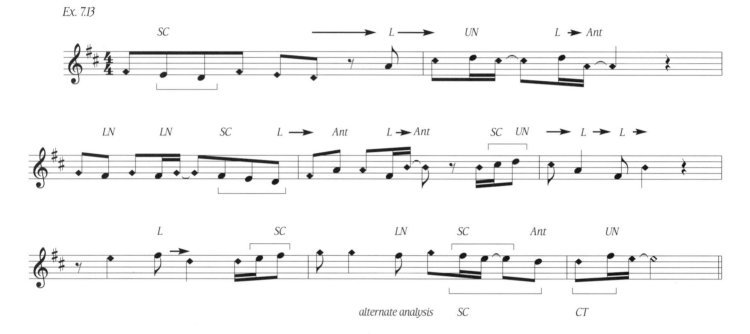

Finding structural tones of the melody is usually fraught with difficult choices. For example, in measure 1, are both the E and D structural tones or is the E only an accented upper neighbor to D? E is metrically strong since it falls on beat 3, but D ends the first part of the phrase. Both notes seem so essential that both are chosen as structural. Measure 5 begins on an eighth note C♯ followed by a quarter note A. Certainly both notes are important, but C♯ is more prominent because it is preceded by pickup notes that direct our attention to it. Also, its stepwise move to B, the next structural tone, is motivically important, being echoed in the next measure by E moving to D. Finally, if the D in the last measure is not considered structural, then it can be seen as part of a changing tone pattern surrounding the final E.

Although you may come to slightly different conclusions as to which notes are structural and which are embellishing, the act of analyzing melody in this manner is ultimately rewarding in that you begin to see the bigger design involved in the construction of melody.

"Can't Take My Eyes Off of You" Many hit songs have melodies made up of little more than melodic step progressions that have been interestingly embellished. Here, the melody slowly descends by step until it reaches the tonic.

Notice that the entire chorus is made up of one rhythmic phrase repeated eight times. The rhyme scheme (aabbccaa) helps avoid over-emphasizing the amount of repetition found in the music.

Ex. 7.14

Can't Take My Eyes Off of You

Words and Music by
Bob Crewe and Bob Gaudio

assignment *Embellishment of the Melodic Outline. "Fill in" or embellish each of the following melodic outlines. Be sure to keep the structural notes structural by placing them in strong metric positions, making them notes of longer values, etc. Label each embellishing tone.*

Ex. 7.15

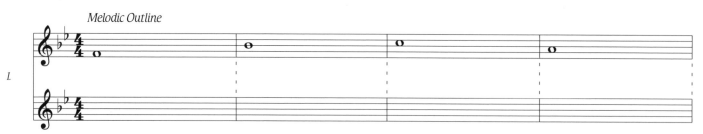

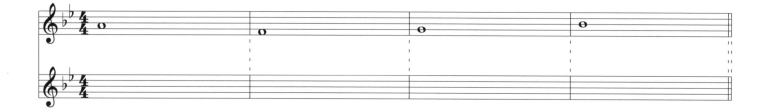

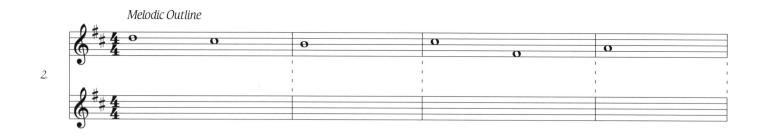

melodic contour There are five basic melodic contours:

1. Ascending

Ex. 7.16

46

2. Descending

Ex. 7.17

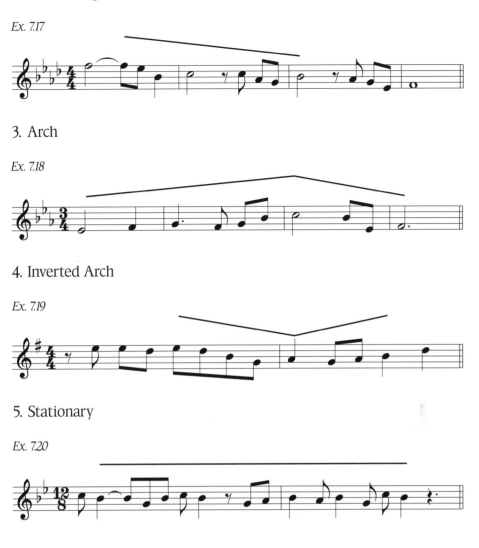

3. Arch

Ex. 7.18

4. Inverted Arch

Ex. 7.19

5. Stationary

Ex. 7.20

Too many phrases with the same contour may cause monotony, as shown in the example below.

Ex. 7.21

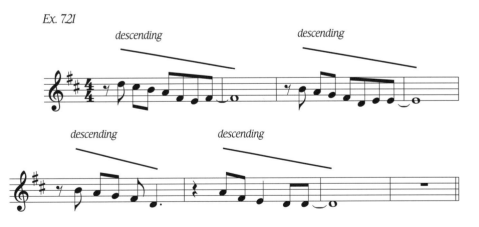

Recognition of the individual phrasal contour as well as recognition of the contour of a combined number of phrases can be very helpful in plotting the course of the melody for a section of a song.

Ex. 7.22

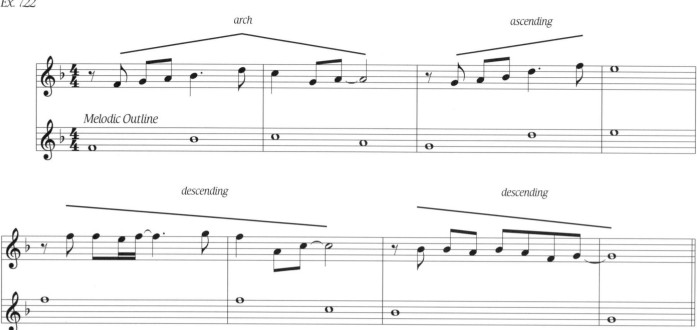

The first two individual phrases are an arch contour followed by an ascending contour. The overall contour of the two combined phrases is an ascending one. This ascending contour is balanced by the next two descending phrases which, when combined with it, show a larger descending design of a large arch contour.

Ex. 7.23

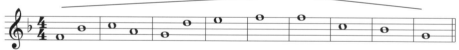

"Because You Loved Me"   Look at the shape or contour of the melody. It is a large arch with a melodic outline mainly made up of melodic step progressions with occasional gaps (the fourth scale degree is missing). Diane Warren did not write an academic-sounding melody with one melodic step following exactly on the heels of another, nor do each of her individual phrases have the exact same contour. Her overall architecture design, the very satisfying arch, is apparent only after study.

The chorus of "Because You Loved Me" (Ex. 7.24) contains seven inexactly matched phrases and one unmatched phrase—the important phrase containing the title.

Phrases in the balancing position are very important because they set up the listener's expectations or contain information that the listener has been set up to receive. Examine the fourth phrase, which is in the balancing position. Its last note is the unstable 2nd degree, which sets up expectations for the resolution to 1 in the last phrase. Also notice that the penultimate phrase ends on 2, again setting up the resolution to 1 in the title phrase.

Ex. 7.24

Because You Loved Me

**Words and Music by
Diane Warren**

assignment *Compose a melody using the given notes as a melodic outline for the overall contours of a section of a song.*

Ex. 7.25 (B minor)

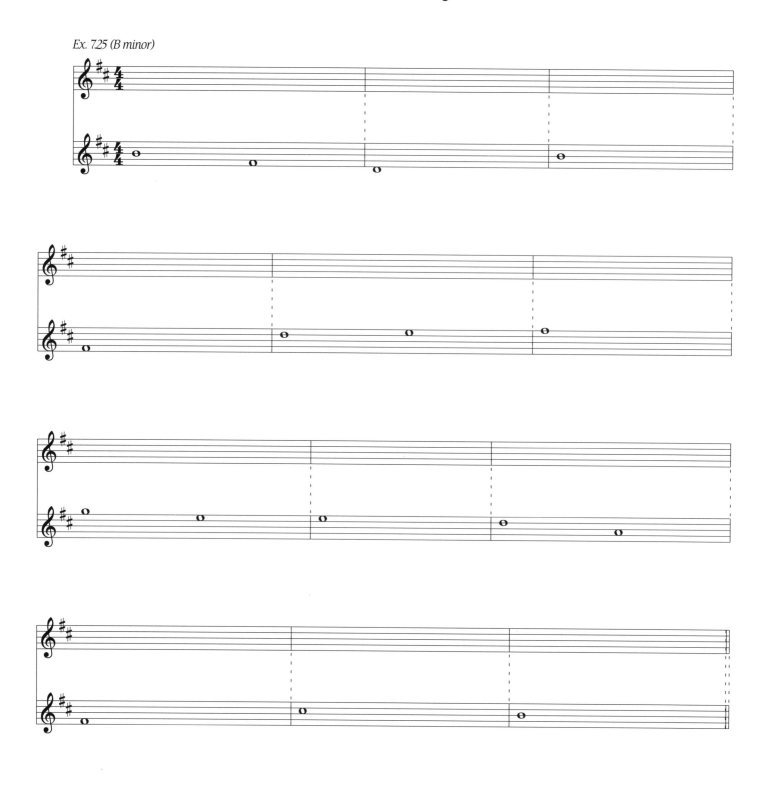

Chapter 8

Controlling the Speed of Your Song

The ability to control the speed of your song allows you to use speed as a structural device, which can be used for contrast and/or for emphasis. There are two ways to control the speed within your song without changing the tempo. You can either

1. Vary the length of the phrases.
2. Vary the rhythms within the phrases.
3. Use (1) and (2) in any combination (e.g., slowing down the phrasal movement while speeding up the rhythms within the phrases).

phrasal acceleration/deceleration

The length of the phrase you start with sets the pace for ensuing phrases and establishes a norm. If the phrase lengths stay the same, the pace is said to be *constant*.

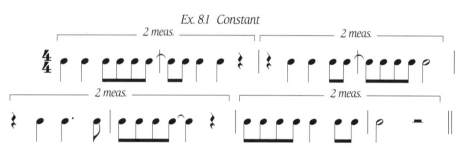

Ex. 8.1 Constant

When phrases move from longer to shorter phrase lengths, they produce *phrasal acceleration.* For instance, a group of two four-bar phrases followed by a group of two two-bar phrases will cause phrasal acceleration. The first two four-bar phrases in the following example set the norm. The next two two-bar phrases create an acceleration. The following four-bar phrase returns to the norm.

Ex. 8.2 Phrasal Acceleration

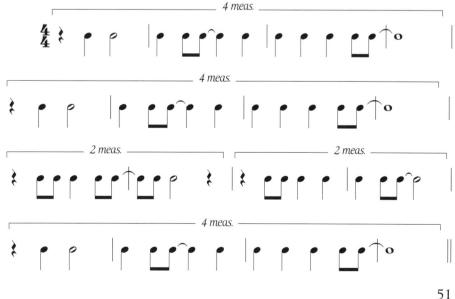

When phrases move from shorter to longer lengths, they produce *phrasal deceleration,* for example, a group of two two-bar phrases followed by one four-bar phrase.

Ex. 8.3 Phrasal Deceleration

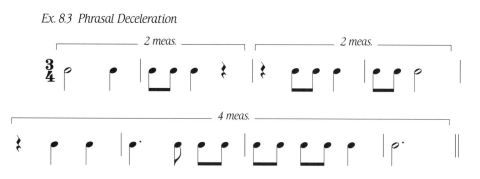

use of phrasal acceleration/deceleration in songwriting

Acceleration or deceleration may be used effectively to create *contrast within a section of a song.* In the following example, deceleration is used to highlight the title line.

Ex. 8.4

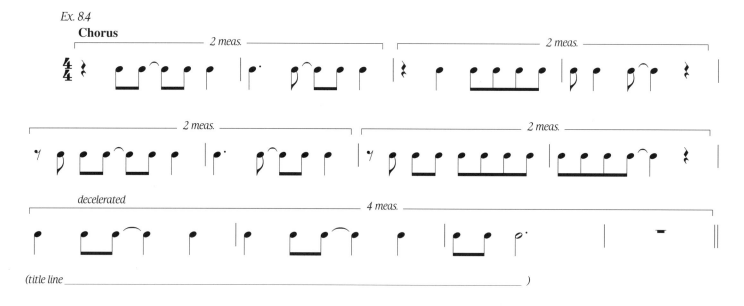

Acceleration or deceleration may also be used to *contrast one section of a song from another section.* In the following example, phrasal acceleration is used to delineate the chorus (which moves approximately in one-measure phrases) from the verse (which moves in four-measure phrases).

Ex. 8.5

A good example of phrasal acceleration occurs in Paul Simon's song, "Fifty Ways to Leave Your Lover," between the verse and chorus sections. The verse section is made up of 2- or 4-measure phrases; the chorus section ("Just slip out the back, Jack") is made up of 1-measure phrases. This gesture heightens the song's prosody of making a fast getaway.

Study the three models below.

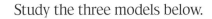

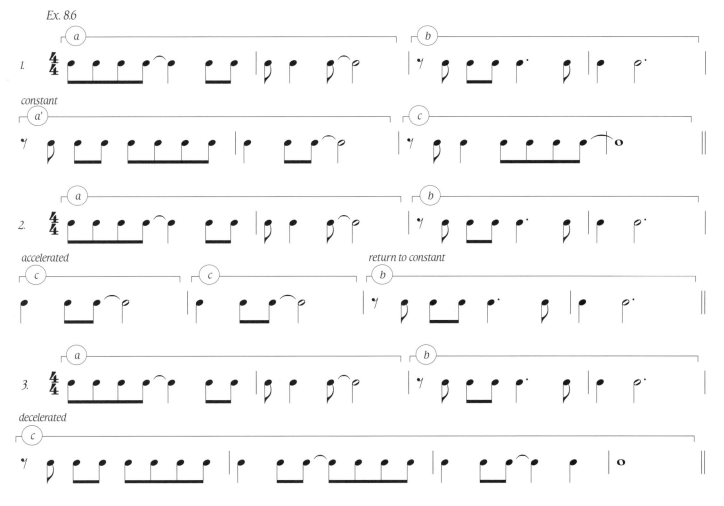

exercise *Using the given phrases as starting points, create the designated movement (constant, accelerated, decelerated) by using either the same, shorter, or longer phrases. Bracket and label each phrase with the appropriate letter.*

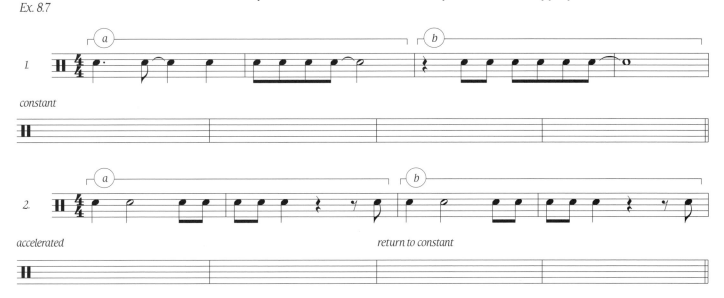

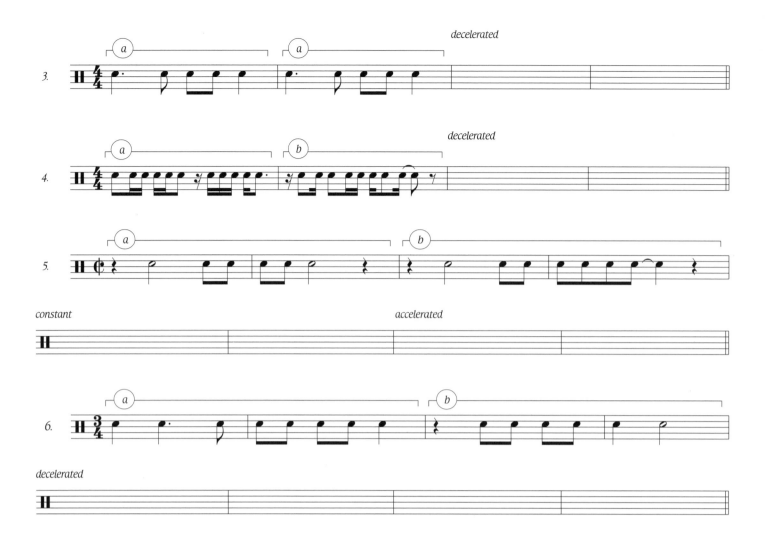

rhythmic acceleration/deceleration

The rhythms you begin with set the pace and establish a norm. If the amount of primary or secondary stresses stays approximately the same within phrases of the same length or within the comparable amount of time, the rhythms are said to be *constant*.

Ex. 8.8 Constant

Rhythmic acceleration is the recognizable difference in movement from a larger rhythmic division to a smaller rhythmic division. Rhythmic acceleration occurs if the amount of primary or secondary stresses increases within phrases of the same length or within the comparable amount of (metric) time.

Ex. 8.9 Rhythmic Acceleration

Rhythmic deceleration is the recognizable difference in movement from a smaller rhythmic division to a larger rhythmic division. Rhythmic deceleration occurs if the amount of primary or secondary stresses decreases within phrases of the same length or within the comparable amount of (metric) time.

Ex. 8.10 Rhythmic Deceleration

Neil Diamond's big hit, "Sweet Caroline," furnishes a fine example of rhythmic deceleration. The verse section mainly contains quarter notes and eighth notes; the pre-chorus contains mainly whole notes and half notes ("Hands... touching hands..."). Deceleration, in this case, produces a tension that gets resolved in the chorus where the type of rhythms that occur in the verse are restored.

Study the three models below.

Ex. 8.II

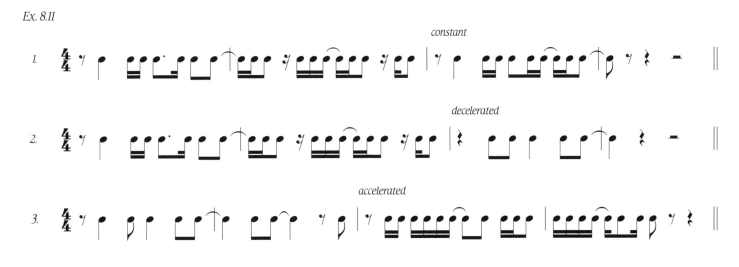

exercise *Create a second phrase that retains the same number of measures as the given phrase but speeds up, slows down, or remains constant based solely on the rhythms within the phrases.*

Ex. 8.II

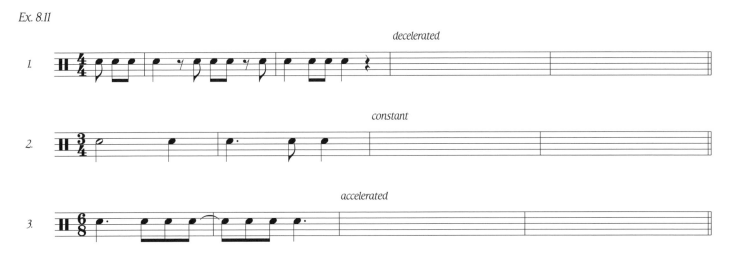

Chapter 9

Melodic Placement

The rhythmic placement of the melody within the measure is a very important aspect of melody writing. Along with other factors that have already been discussed in detail (such as the rhythm of the phrases and melodic cadences), studying the following should lead you to a more complete understanding of the consequences involved when you choose where melodic phrases begin and end.

phrase endings The most obvious or natural cessation point for a melodic phrase is at a strong cadential point. Strong cadential points are areas within the metric phrase where rhythmic activity most comfortably stops. Again, symmetry determines that area. The strongest cadential point is found on the first beat of the last half of the metric phrase. It is on that beat that a symmetric occurrence of the phrase just heard would take place if it were to be repeated.

In a two-bar phrase, the strongest cadential point is beat 1 of the second measure.

Ex. 9.1a

In a four-bar phrase, the strongest cadential point is beat 1 of the third measure.

Ex. 9.1b

The second strongest cadential point is the first beat of the last fourth of the metric phrase, such as the third beat, second measure in a two-bar phrase,

Ex. 9.2a

or the first beat, fourth measure in a four-bar phrase.

Ex. 9.2b

As a composer, you must decide how conclusive a stop is needed in various phrases and sections of your song. If you want a very conclusive stop, you would choose to stop at the strongest cadential point; if you want your phrase to end in a less conclusive manner, you would stop at a weak cadential area. Examine the following:

Ex. 9.3a

The rather stiff start-stop effect found in the phrases in the example below is caused by the cessation of melodic motion on the same cadential point.

Ex. 9.3b

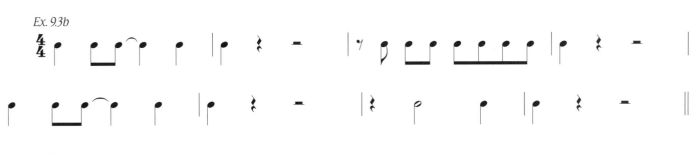

By altering the ending of some phrases, a more fluid or "conversational" rhythmic flow is achieved, as shown below.

Ex. 9.3c

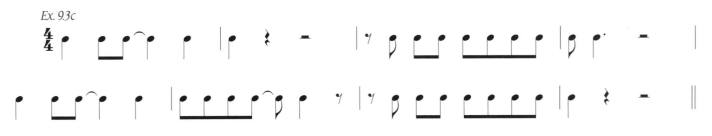

phrase beginnings   Most melodic phrases begin either on the first beat or soon thereafter.

Ex. 9.4

pickup notes If one or two notes (usually not longer than a beat) lead into the first beat, they are considered *pickup notes.* Pickup notes highlight or emphasize the note on the first beat.

Ex. 9.5

beginning on the weak part of the measure or metric grouping Some melodic phrases don't begin and end within the confines of obvious barlines.

Ex. 9.6

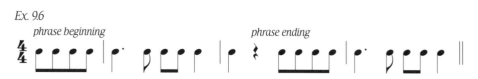

The first half of each measure or metric grouping is stronger than the second half. (For example, in a two-measure phrase, the first measure is strong, the second measure is weak.) Beginning on the weak part of the measure or metric grouping tends to create interest by focusing attention on a metric area not usually emphasized. Study the rhythms in the following example and notice how interest is created when the melody breaks away from the constant two-measure phrase structure and begins on both the weak part of the phrase (the second bar of what "normally" would have been a two-bar phrase) and the weak part of the measure (the second half of the measure).

Ex. 9.7

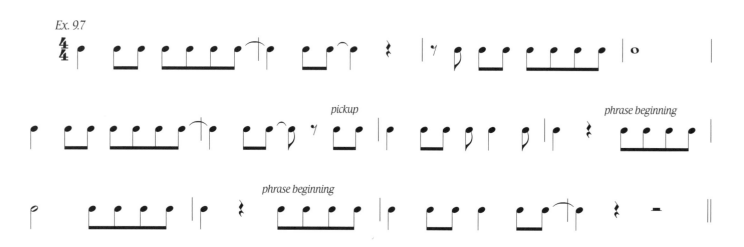

You should be especially aware of the starting point of each phrase in a given section of a song so that a contrast may be created either within that section or, more importantly, to another section.

"Love Is You" Examine the melody on the following page and notice where each phrase begins and ends. Especially notice how the first line of the chorus, "Love is new," begins on the weak measure of a two-measure phrase and arrives on the first beat of the chorus and, by doing so, highlights it. (The arrows point to phrases that begin on the weak part of the measure.)

Ex. 9.8

Love Is You

Words by Denise Utt
Music by Jack Perricone

Chapter 10

Building Sections

Your decisions in building any section of music will involve each of the compositional variables. At this point in the study, we will consider only the first five of the compositional variables in building a section of music:

1. The number of phrases: Symmetrical/Asymmetrical
2. The length of the phrases: Balanced/Unbalanced
   [Constant/Accelerated/Decelerated]
3. The rhythm of the phrases: Balanced/Unbalanced
   [Constant/Accelerated/Decelerated]
4. The order of the phrases: Symmetrical/Asymmetrical
5. Cadential melodic pitch: Stable/Unstable
6. Harmonic cadences

Compositional Variables 1 to 3 have previously been discussed in detail. The *order of the phrases,* presented below, is a very important variable when we attempt to build a section of music.

the order of the phrases
The order in which phrases appear helps define whether the section is symmetric or asymmetric. An *aabb* or an *abab* order will give us a symmetric section, whereas an *abba* order will give us an asymmetric section.

building a symmetric section
Keep in mind that *the number of phrases* in a section also helps determine whether a section is symmetric or asymmetric. An even number of phrases of the same length will cause the section to be balanced. An *aaaa* section is symmetric (it has an even number of phrases), whereas an *aaa* section is asymmetric (it has an odd number of phrases).

aaaa
Let's begin simply by building a symmetric section. We'll keep it as simple as possible by using only one phrase, two measures in length, containing the same rhythm but different pitches. Since the phrase is always the same except for the element of pitch, pitch must be wisely used to keep the phrase moving and interesting.

Ex. 10.1 Rhythm Alone

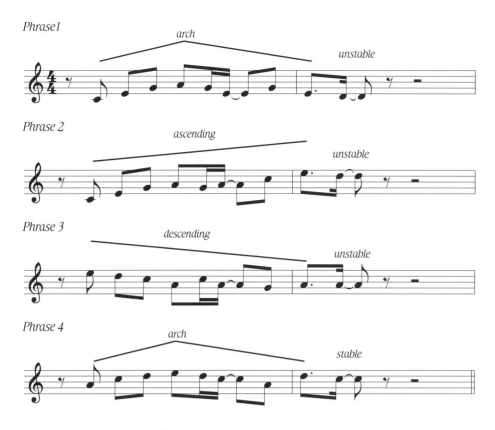

Phrase 1

Phrase 2

Phrase 3

Phrase 4

Notice that phrase 2 begins like phrase 1 but changes melodic contour. Phrase 3 retains continuity with phrase 2 by beginning on the last two notes of the previous phrase and by using a descending contour to balance the previous phrase's ascending one. Phrase 4 rises to the unstable 2nd degree (the unstable 2nd degree also ended phrase 1 and phrase 2), which finally resolves to the tonic note at the end of the phrase.

a b a b The *abab* structure is one of the most common found in popular song. It, too, builds a completely symmetric section. When we use the rhythmic structure of the ⓐ and ⓑ phrases previously exposed, a 16-measure section is created.

Ex. 10.2 Rhythm Alone

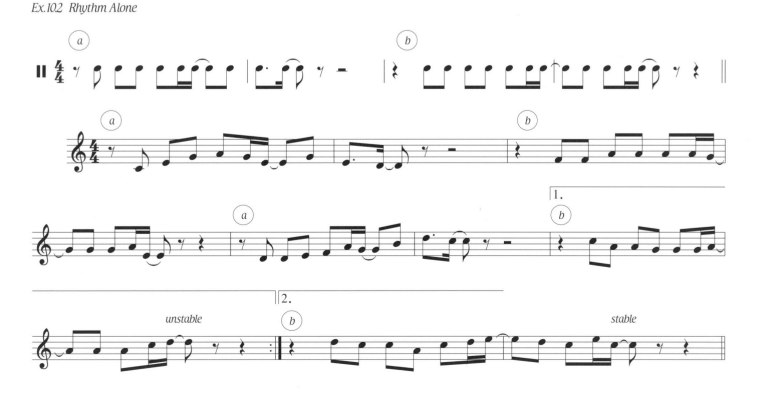

Notice that the section does not close tonally at the first ending due to the unstable last note. The entire piece then repeats except for the last phrase (the second ending). There, it closes completely due to the ending on the tonic note.

an asymmetric, balanced section: a a b b

The *aabb* phrase order produces an asymmetric structure that has two rhythmic closures. The danger this presents is that the music may have a stop-and-go quality. This can be ameliorated by keeping the ends of phrases tonally open. If the last melodic pitch of a phrase is unstable, then that element alone will keep the section somewhat open.

Ex.10.3 aabb

The example now appears with its fourth phrase rewritten. Notice that complete closure is ensured by placing the tonic as the final note.

Ex.10.4

building a balanced but not perfectly symmetric section: a a b a

A section made up of a group of phrases in an *aaba* order does not set up strong expectations. The second (a) phrase balances the first, fragmenting the section. When the (b) occurs, the listener realizes something new has arrived but doesn't know what is to follow (since no expectations have been set up), so that when (a) returns in the balancing position, the closure sounds quite natural.

Ex. 10.5

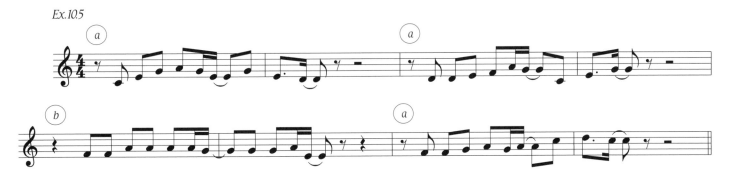

a b a a

An *abaa* ordering of a section is more demanding of a listener's expectations than the previous example. After hearing (a) (b) followed by (a), the listener expects to hear another (b). When another (a) occurs, the listener's expectations are thwarted. The last (a) does, however, effectively close the section, since it is the fourth phrase and balances the previous (a). The closure is, therefore, deceptive. Deceptive closures (whether rhythmic or tonal) are one of the best ways in which songwriters, lyricists, and composers create interest and, possibly, delight our listeners.

Ex. 10.6

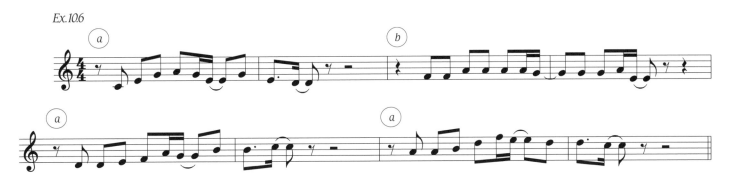

a a a b

An *aaab* ordering of the phrases is balanced but obviously asymmetric. As my ditty indicates, it focuses the listener's attention on the last line. Notice that the matched rhythms and rhymes of the first three phrases focus even more attention on the last phrase (which neither matches nor rhymes). This structure is especially effective when writing a verse/refrain form with the refrain at the end of the verse or when writing a chorus with the title at the end of the chorus. A fine example of this strategy is found in Diane Warren's song, "Because You Loved Me," pages 48–49.

Ex.10.7

a

I've tried to keep this tune __ mel - od - ic. __

a   *a*

It's hard - ly what you'd call __ rhap - sod - ic. __   It's not in - spired but it's __ meth -

b

od - ic, __   de - signed to em - pha - size a ti - tle or re - frain. _

open or closed?   After hearing the last example, you may feel that although the order of the phrases is asymmetric, the total effect of this section is closed. Let's look more closely at the compositional variables to analyze what is tending to close the section and what is tending to keep the section open:

1. The number of phrases: Symmetrical
2. Phrase lengths: Constant
3. Rhythm of the phrases: Constant
4. The order of the phrases: Asymmetrical
5. Cadential melodic pitch: Stable

We now can comprehend why the section sounds somewhat closed. It is only the order of the phrases that keeps the section slightly open and somewhat interesting (possibly interesting enough to allow the entire section to repeat).

creating open sections   Sections of songs meant to lead to the central idea, for instance, a verse or transitional bridge leading to either a chorus or refrain, tend to be somewhat open. That does not mean all the compositional variables must be open. In fact, many songs contain verses that are symmetric and closed in all but the melodic and harmonic instability of the last cadence before the central idea. (See Ex.10.8 containing an *abab* order.)

Ex.10.8

unbalancing a section Unbalancing a section creates a sense of movement and tension that seeks resolution. It is an especially useful device to employ when writing verse sections or transitional bridge sections—sections whose main function is to lead to the central idea.

It is possible to unbalance a section in any number of ways. The means demonstrated in Ex. 10.9 are just some of the ways this can be done.

1. Shortening the last phrase (unbalancing the number of measures per phrase), thereby causing an acceleration into the next section (see first and second endings). Compositional variable used to unbalance section: *length of the phrases.*

2. Lengthening the last phrase (unbalancing the number of measures per phrase), thereby decelerating the momentum. This deceleration frustrates the listener's expectations, causing him to focus on the next section (see third and fourth endings). Compositional variable used to unbalance section: *length of the phrases.*

3. Adding a phrase and, in addition, shortening the last phrase to cause an acceleration into the next section (see fifth ending). Compositional variables used to unbalance section: *number of phrases and length of the phrases.*

Notice that (1) the order of the sections is not symmetric (the fourth ending does yield an *abab* order, but the added two beats of rest effectively unbalance the structure), and (2) each section ends on an unstable pitch, which, of course, helps the section to be open.

Ex. 10.9

creating interesting
balanced sections

Most *A* sections in *AABA* songs and most *chorus* sections in verse/chorus songs contain the central idea of the song. (See Chapter Twelve for definitions of these song forms.) Unlike verse or transitional bridge sections in verse/chorus songs, whose purpose is to lead to the central idea, sections that contain the central idea (often the title) are summational or declarative. Because of this, these sections tend to be balanced. There are, however, many additional ways of building sections that may be imperfect in their symmetry but that still produce a sense of balance within the section.

The possibilities for creating an interesting balanced section are as infinite as one's imagination. The following examples are possible balanced sections, not models that must be stringently adhered to.

Ex.10.10 abcca

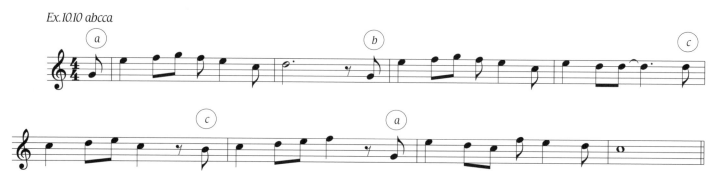

Retaining the initial musical idea established by the first phrase, I then create a second phrase, (b), which retains the exact pitch of the (a) phrase for its first measure but extends into the upbeat of three in its second measure. The following two (c) phrases are also derived from the initial idea, which is now truncated, reducing each phrase to one measure. This phrasal acceleration produces tension and focuses attention on the last phrase. The last phrase provides release in two ways: by returning to a two-bar structure and by concluding on the tonic note.

This section is not symmetrical (the order of the phrases is asymmetrical; the number of phrases is asymmetrical), but it is balanced. Each phrase or phrase grouping has a phrase or phrase grouping that balances it: (a) (two measures) is balanced by (b) (two measures) and the two (c) phrases (one measure each) are balanced by the final (a) (two measures) phrase.

66

A balanced section with these characteristics can be very useful. Consider that the (a) phrases could easily contain the title, placing it both as the first and the last thing heard in the chorus. The end rhymes (i.e., *unfold, old*) of the (c) phrases heighten the tension caused by phrasal acceleration and further help focus attention on the last phrase.

Ex.10.11

I'll al-ways re-mem-ber to-day   'cause you made it spe-cial in ev-'ry way.   As

our lives un-fold   this day   won't grow old.   I'll al-ways re-mem-ber to-day.

a b a / a b a   The following example is another attempt to create a longer balanced section. The first part of the section consists of three phrases, (a) (b) (a'). Each of the phrases is two measures long. They are followed by a matched set of phrases, (a) (b) (a'), which effectively closes the section. This section, you may have noticed, is 12 measures in length rather than the usual eight.

Ex.10.12

fragmentation

The concept of "open" and "closed" is extremely important. Once you understand this concept, it will help you with many aspects of writing songs: combining pitch with rhythm to form melody, combining melody with harmony, and combining music with lyrics.

Since all elements of a song need not close at the same time, strategies involving rhythmic closure but tonal openness can be employed in sections of a song to either propel one section to another or to focus the listener's attention on an important phrase. When there is an internal point of rhythmic resolution within a section, the structure is said to be *fragmented.*

The following verse/chorus structures contain fragmentation points. In other words, there are places within each section where the structure is rhythmically closed and that could have completely closed if they were not kept open tonally.

Quite often a verse section closes rhythmically, but not tonally. The next phrase after the fragmentation point serves to unbalance the section and often provides a powerful lead-in to the chorus.

Ex.10.13a

68

The chorus that follows this verse contains two sections that are fragmented. The first occurs in measure 8, at the end of the second b phrase. The fragmentation causes us to hear the chorus in sections. (We will call these eight measures the A section of the chorus, the next eight measures the B section of the chorus, and the last four measures the C section of the chorus.)

The second fragmentation occurs in measure 16, at the end of the b' phrase. Here the structure is completely balanced (eight measures plus eight measures) with the b' phrase providing the expected rhythmic closure.

The same kind of phrase strategy that occurred in the verse after the fragmentation point can occur in a chorus structure, the difference being that the last phrase (which sounds and feels like an added phrase) usually closes tonally to satisfy listener expectations. Note how the final phrase provides a great opportunity for an important lyric or for the title.

Ex.10.13b

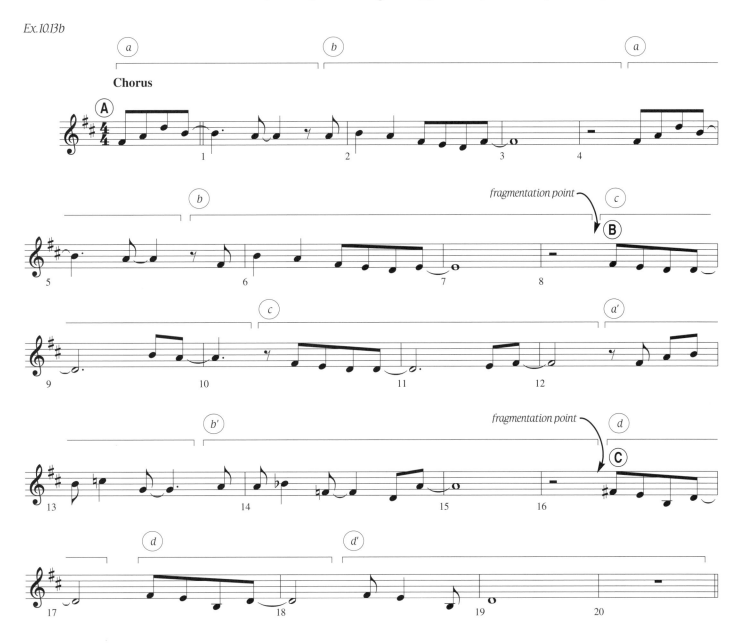

69

Here is the entire music for the song, including chord symbols. Play it so you can feel the various places where the music fragments, how harmony helps keep the song open, and how it also helps to close it.

In order for you to better understand the importance of structural choices, I've rewritten the song, deleting the added phrases (which had occurred after the fragmentation points) and making each section a balanced, rhythmically closed structure. I think you will agree with me in perceiving these structures as much duller.

Ex.10.13d

assignment

1. Compose pitches to the given rhythms to create an *aaaa* eight-measure section.

Ex. 10.14

2. Compose pitches to the following rhythms to create an *abab* eight-measure section that ends open; then, using a second ending, create eight additional measures that effectively close the section.

Ex. 10.15

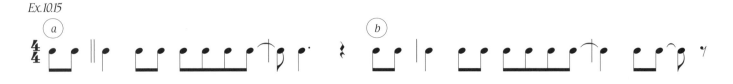

3. Create an unbalanced section, 7 to 16 measures in length, by any of the methods demonstrated under the heading "Unbalancing a Section." Label the rhythm of the phrases and describe the method you've chosen to unbalance the section.

4. Create a simple eight-measure balanced section of music; close it rhythmically to cause it to fragment, but keep it open tonally. Then add a phrase to the section to close it tonally. (You may use chords in this assignment.)

Chapter 11
Developmental Techniques

motive

The smallest unit of music that embodies enough of a shape and rhythm to be identifiable is called a *motive*. A motive achieves its identity through repetition, whether literal or varied, and is often used as the main building block of a composition.[*]

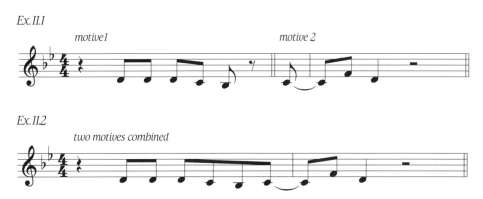

Ex.11.1

motive1　　　　　　　　　　　*motive 2*

Ex.11.2

two motives combined

variety within unity

Repetition is possibly the most important factor in making anything memorable. Yet repetition without variation causes monotony. Too much variation (change) causes incoherence. If you want to produce music that is both coherent and interesting, the knowledge of developmental techniques is of paramount importance.

developmental technique #1: retain the rhythmic structure, change the pitch

One of the most basic and useful developmental techniques is to retain the rhythmic structure of the phrases but to change the pitch content and/or the contour of the phrase.

In the following example, the rhythmic structure of the first two-measure phrase is retained throughout the succeeding six measures. In measures 3–4, the first three pitches of the original phrase are retained, but the contour of the phrase has been changed. In measures 5–6, the arch contour established in measures 3–4 has been retained, but the pitches have been changed. The phrase beginning of measures 7–8 retains the first note of the previous phrase but then changes both the pitch content and the contour of the phrase. (See Ex 11.3 on the next page.)

---

[*] The motive is sometimes referred to, in general, as an "idea."

Ex.II.3

sequence A sequence is a more exacting form of the developmental technique just described. In other words, the rhythmic structure and the intervallic structure are retained while the pitch level is changed. Sequences may be *exact*, with both the size of the intervals and the quality of the intervals kept the same, or *inexact*, with the size of the interval retained but with the quality of the interval changed.

Because the size and the quality of the intervals are retained, the exact sequence is often found in passages that modulate.

Ex.II.4 Exact Sequence

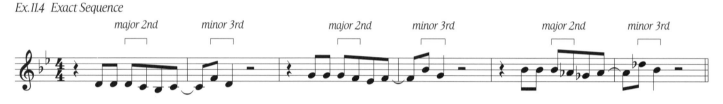

The inexact sequence is frequently employed to retain the same tonality and to remain strictly diatonic.

Ex.II.5 Inexact Sequence

assignment *Create an eight-measure section of music in which each phrase retains the rhythmic structure of the given phrase but changes the pitch content and/or the contour of the phrase.*

Ex.II.6

Moderate rock

Moderately slow rock ballad

Sequence the following phrases, making sure that the sequence remains diatonic in the original key. Indicate if the sequence is exact or inexact. If inexact, indicate where a different quality of interval was needed for the music to retain its original tonality.

use of developmental technique #1 in the compositional process

One of the most helpful activities you can pursue when composing is thoroughly examining original ideas to seek out their potential.

Ex. II.8

The phrase is made up of two motives. Motive 2 is similar to motive 1 and could be said to be derived from it. Wouldn't it be possible to separate and develop one or the other?

Ex. II.9

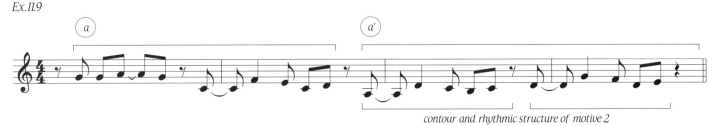

This second phrase in Ex. II.9 is created by retaining the rhythmic structure and contour of motive 2, but beginning each repetition at a different pitch level. Now the first full phrase can bear repetition.

Ex. II.10

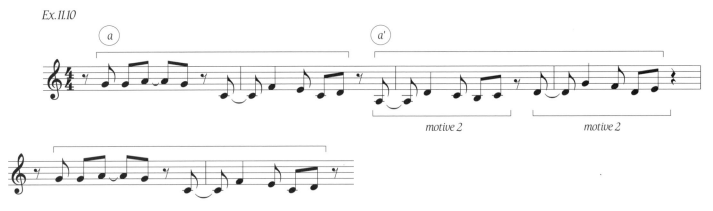

A repetition of the second phrase would be too predictable and monotonous, so why not use the techniques of retaining the rhythm and changing the pitch content?

Ex. II.11

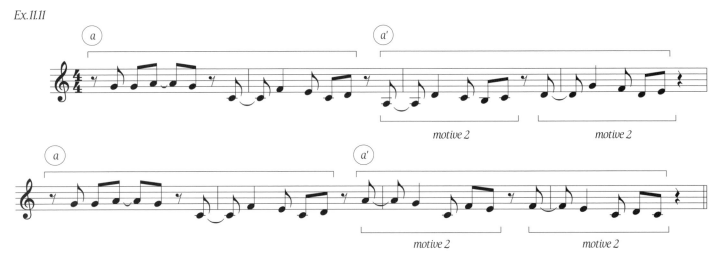

This section is now quite satisfying with enough variety and with unity ensured, since all of the material is derived from the original motives. The successive repetition of motive 2 provides an acceleration.

developmental technique #2: varying the phrase structure; extension and truncation

Another technique frequently used to develop an idea is to change either the length of the phrase or the rhythm of the phrase while retaining the motivic ideas presented in the initial statement. In order to change the rhythmic phrase structure, the motive may undergo either an extension (adding rhythmic value) or a truncation (subtracting rhythmic value).

Ex.11.12

Notice in Ex. 11.12 that both the rhythm of the phrase and the length of the phrase have been extended.

Ex.11.13

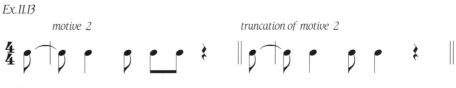

Notice in Ex. 11.13 that only the rhythm of the phrase has been truncated.

Ex.11.14 Development Using an Extension of Motive1

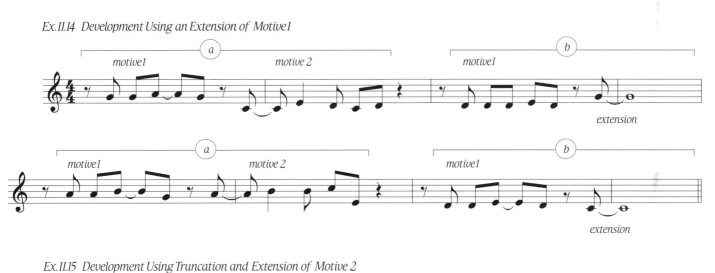

Ex.11.15 Development Using Truncation and Extension of Motive 2

assignment 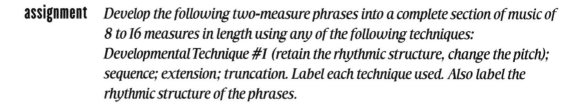 *Develop the following two-measure phrases into a complete section of music of 8 to 16 measures in length using any of the following techniques: Developmental Technique #1 (retain the rhythmic structure, change the pitch); sequence; extension; truncation. Label each technique used. Also label the rhythmic structure of the phrases.*

Ex. 11.16

Write an original two-measure phrase. Develop it into a complete section of music using the methods described. Label the techniques used and also label the rhythmic structure of the phrases.

3.

developmental techniques   The following developmental techniques are found in all types of music composition, not just songs. Sometimes they are used as they are presented below—in their pristine form—but more often they are used together in two or more combinations, integrated with each other in interesting ways, sometimes making it difficult to name the exact developmental techniques employed. This should not present a problem to you because your concern as a composer is not analysis, but creativity.

The human mind tends to permutate and transform any set of fairly complex raw materials (how many times have you permutated a telephone number?) and rejoice in the wonders of these transformations. This process is the life-blood of music-making. Learn these individually presented techniques; practice them and eventually you will see and hear them in what you write.

Ex. II.17 Original Motives

1. Repetition—simply repeats the motive or phrase.

Ex. II.18

2. Rhythmic Retention/Pitch Change (previously referred to as Developmental Technique #1)—retains the rhythm of the motive or phrase but changes the pitches.

Ex. II.19

3. Sequence—repeats the motive or phrase at a different pitch level. Sequences may be exact (same quality intervals) or inexact (same size, different quality).

Ex. II.20

4. Extension—adds new material to the motive or phrase usually at the end, though it is possible to add new material at the beginning and/or in the middle.

Ex. II.21

5. Truncation—shortens the motive or phrase.

Ex. II.22

6. Inversion—inverts the intervals of the motive or phrase. (Most inversions are inexact in order to remain diatonic in the original key.)

Ex. II.23

7. Retrograde—presents the motive or phrase backwards.

Ex. II.24

(retrograde of motive 2)

8. Diminution—shortens the note values.

Ex. II.25

9. Augmentation—lengthens the note values.

Ex. II.26

10. Segmentation—uses only a portion of the motive or the phrase. This technique is very similar to truncation, the only difference being one of degree and usage. If only a very small part of a phrase is isolated from it, we refer to it as a fragment.

Ex. II.27

11. Permutation—changes the note order.

Ex. II.28

12. Interversion—presents the motives of a phrase in a different order: a/b becomes b/a.

Ex. II.29

13. Conjunction—new material (usually one or two notes) that connects two motives or two phrases together.

Ex. II.30

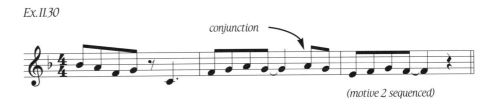

14. Ornamentation—retains all the main notes of a motive or phrase but embellishes them.

Ex. II.31

15. Thinning—is the opposite of ornamentation, involving the deletion of certain notes of a motive or a phrase, leaving the overall length the same.

Ex. II.32

16. Rhythmic Displacement—is the placement of a motive or phrase in a different metric or rhythmic area than the one in which it originally appeared.

Ex. II.33

17. Elision (Dovetailing)—is the joining together of two phrases, usually by having the last note of the first phrase become the first note of the next phrase. Elision always implies deletion. For example, a four-measure phrase that contains a three-measure melody followed by a one-measure rest could be elided to the following phrase by eliminating the one-measure rest.

Ex.II.34

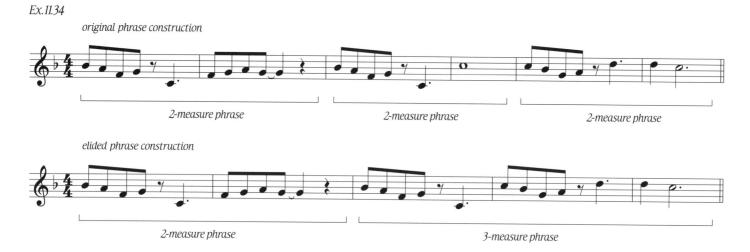

original phrase construction

2-measure phrase   2-measure phrase   2-measure phrase

elided phrase construction

2-measure phrase   3-measure phrase

Elision can be obvious to your audience or, as in this case, somewhat hidden. In its hidden state, it is still a very powerful tool that can elevate and enliven your compositions.

elision of motives a and b

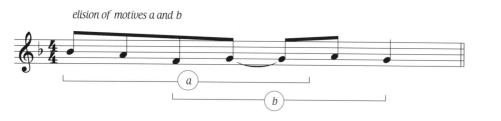

a

b

assignment   *Develop the following two-measure phrase as indicated.*

1. Compose a diatonic sequence beginning a half-step higher.

Ex.II.35

2. Extend the sequence by at least one measure (refer to #1).

Ex.II.36

3. *Truncate the sequence (refer to #1).*

Ex.II.37

4. *Compose two additional measures using only a rhythmic fragment of the melodic figure.*

Ex.II.38

5. *Compose a rhythmically matched phrase that does not have the same contour as the original melody.*

Ex.II.39

6. *Invert the given phrase.*

Ex.II.40

7. *Compose an additional two or more measures of music that rhythmically displace a motive from the original phrase.*

Ex.II.41

8. *Use a conjunction to make the two two-measure phrases into one four-measure phrase.*

Ex.II.42

9. *Develop the motives into a 16-to 24-measure section of a song by any means defined in this lesson. Where possible, label each technique or combination of techniques employed. This exercise may be done on a separate piece of manuscript paper.*

Ex. II.43

Chapter 12

Form

The control and perception of form in any music involves recognition of two basic musical activities—repetition (or similarity) and change (or contrast)—plus an activity that combines these two. This latter activity is referred to as "development" and provides contrast within similarity. In this grey area, it is sometimes difficult to distinguish and designate one section from another. Some of the factors that help us differentiate one section from another are as follows:

1. Closure: either phrasal, rhythmic, melodic, or harmonic. (The degree of closure is directly related to the number of elements closing simultaneously.)
2. The treatment of the tonality (e.g., diatonic vs. chromatic).
3. The length of the phrases.
4. The rhythm of the phrases.
5. The melodic contour.
6. The tessitura* and/or range.

Play and/or sing the following song. Notice where the song sectionalizes and what elements are causing the second section to sound different from the first section.

Ex.12.1

---

* Tessitura means the position of pitches within the melodic range (low, medium, high).

85

In the previous example, the listener expects a change to occur after the second ending (measure 16). This is caused by a number of elements in the music concluding or closing at this point:

1. The phrase structure. The phrase structure becomes completely symmetric at measure 16.
2. The tonality. The melody concludes on the tonic note; the harmony concludes on the tonic chord.

The section of music that follows does not greatly contrast with the previous section in all its elements. To be more specific, the melodic rhythm of the song remains pretty much the same throughout and the phrase lengths are mainly two measures long. What, then, does contrast?

1. The treatment of the tonality in this new section is quite different from that in the previous section. The harmony, which for 16 measures had remained diatonic, suddenly becomes chromatic. The first section states the tonality by both beginning and ending with the tonic chord. The second section avoids the tonal center by using secondary dominant chords and by never stating the tonic chord.
2. Another more subtle change is the melodic contour and range of the melody. In the first section, the melody does not move too far from the notes of the opening phrase, the tessitura of the section occurring in the medium-low to medium range. In the second section, the melody rises gradually over a number of measures to the highest notes of the song and then gradually falls, encompassing more than an octave within its nine measures.
3. An added measure at the end of the second section produces a welcome asymmetry that helps propel this section back to the beginning of the song and provides a healthy contrast to the predominantly two-bar phrase structure.

song forms   The forms found in popular songs are generally simple. Most popular songs last three to four minutes and contain sections that repeat. The number of sections vary from one to four.

the central statement   Common to most popular songs, no matter what specific form they take, is the goal area, which we refer to as the central statement or central idea. The central statement can be the title, the refrain, the hook (a term that generally means an extremely memorable melodic/lyric phrase [usually the title]) or simply an area of the song that contains very important lyric and musical content.

Song form can be conceived and analyzed as either *leading to* the central statement or as being *derived from* the central statement.

song sections: **the verse**	The verse is the section of the song that spins out the story, that furthers the action. The lyric of the verse is composed of a series of lines arranged in a recurring pattern. The number of lines, the meter, and rhyme scheme of the lyric in a verse, once stated, is fixed; only the content is changed. The music of the verse, once stated, remains fixed.
the refrain	The refrain of a song is the central idea, either the title or a line containing the title, or a very important lyric that occurs as part of each verse. Although a refrain can begin a verse, it more commonly ends each verse (or ends a series of verses). The refrain is *not* a separate section of a song; it is always part of the verse. Note: the term *refrain* was and still is used in some published music to mean what we call the chorus. All songwriting courses at the Berklee College of Music and most contemporary music publishers use the term as we have defined it.
the chorus	The chorus of a verse/chorus song is a section of the song that usually contains the central statement (title or hook). This section repeats *both* words and music.
the bridge	The term itself implies a section that connects two other sections. This, in fact, is the main purpose of any bridge. It may also have other functions, for example, to provide contrast or to modulate. The term "bridge," without any prefix, refers to a section of a song that occurs *after* the central statement, for instance, after a refrain or after the *AA* section in a "standard" form *AABA* song (the *B* section of a standard form *AABA* song is the bridge).
transitional bridge	A transitional bridge is a linking section, usually between verse and chorus. Its function is to lead up to or build up a momentum to the chorus. Sometimes the transitional bridge is followed by a refrain instead of a chorus, but its function remains the same. The transitional bridge is always found before the central statement. Note: the term *transitional bridge* is a Berklee College of Music term coined because no adequate name existed for this section of a song. Sheila Davis, in her book *The Craft of Lyric Writing,* calls this same section the "climb"; others refer to it as the "pre-chorus" or "pre-hook."
primary bridge	A primary bridge is found in verse/chorus songs after the chorus section and, most usually, after the second chorus has been stated. It provides contrast or relief from previously heard sections and prepares a return (sometimes with a modulation) to either the verse or chorus. Note: the term *primary bridge* is a Berklee College of Music term coined to differentiate it from the term *transitional bridge.*

frequently encountered song forms

The following forms are those most often encountered in popular songs. The list is neither totally inclusive nor conclusive. As I've tried to indicate, *form is often a result of continual compositional decisions, rather than a predetermined pattern by which you are forced to mold your song.* It is wise, however, to be aware of the most common forms, especially if you are aiming your songs at the commercial song marketplace. Common forms are useful. Ultimately, it is what you put in them that counts. Keep in mind that it is the taste of the wine that matters; after all, most wine bottles have the same shape!

Most commonly found in folk music, the *AAA* form is simply one in which the music, once stated, is repeated again and again, each time with a different set of lyrics.

AAA

‖: **verse** :‖   (number of repeats determined by lyric considerations)

Verse/refrain

‖: **verse/refrain** :‖   (repeats determined by lyric considerations)

Verse/refrain with bridge

‖ **verse/refrain** | **verse/refrain** ‖ **bridge** ‖ **verse/refrain** ‖

Verse/chorus

‖: **verse** | **chorus** :‖

Verse; transitional bridge, chorus

‖: **verse** | **transitional bridge** | **chorus** :‖

Verse, chorus with primary bridge

‖ **verse** | **chorus** ‖ **verse** | **chorus** ‖ **primary bridge** ‖: **chorus** :‖

Verse, chorus with both transitional and primary bridges

‖: **verse** | **transitional bridge** | **chorus** :‖ **primary bridge** ‖: **chorus** :‖

the "standards" song form

The "standards" type of song, written mainly between 1920 and 1950, is still the mainstay of theater songwriting. The focus of this form is placed on the chorus because the dramatic action on stage usually doesn't require a verse to tell the story; instead, the writers usually need a section of music to move from dialogue into full-blown song. This is provided by an introductory verse.

the introductory verse

An introductory verse is usually stated only once and functions as an introduction to the main body of the song, the chorus. The length and form of the introductory verse vary greatly and are dependent upon each individual dramatic situation.

the chorus The chorus of the "standards" type of song is the *whole song* divorced from its introductory verse. There are a number of formats that this "standards" type usually utilizes. The most frequent is the *AABA* in which the first section *A*, containing the central statement, is repeated and followed by a contrasting section *B* known as the bridge (also referred to as the "release"), which then returns to the first section *A*. The *A* section usually contains the title, which appears either at the beginning or at the end of it.[*]

Another format for the chorus of a "standards" type of song is the *ABAB^I* or *ABAC* a form that is characterized by the lack of a complete closure of the *A* section, with the climax of the song usually occurring in the *B^I* or *C* section. The *ABAB^I* is similar to the *ABAC*. When the *B* section is repeated, it is usually slightly altered to make a suitable ending.

The lack of a complete closure of the A section causes this form to be heard in two large sections: ‖ *A B* | *A B^I (or C)* ‖. *B* and *B^I* or *C* aren't meant to contrast drastically with the *A* section and *do not* function as a *bridge*; rather, they are meant to add variety, usually by developing materials already presented in the A section.

The 32-measure "standards" chorus tends to be balanced, especially in the number of measures in each section. If the *A* section in an *AABA* chorus is eight measures long, then it and its repetition yield 16 measures. If the *B* section is also eight measures long and is followed by the last *A* section (another eight measures), then these last two sections (16 measures) perfectly balance the first two sections. The *ABAC* or *ABAB^I* choruses also tend to be balanced because the *B* section (or *B^I* or *C* sections) are usually the same number of measures as the *A* section.

Note that although most songs written in the era of the "standards" song form were 32 measures long, many exceptions exist. Composers such as Cole Porter, Harold Arlen, Leonard Bernstein and Stephen Sondheim stretched choruses well beyond 32 measures

the concept of open and closed and its relationship to form One of the most interesting aspects of composing a song is the control of how open or closed a section is to be. Not all elements need be uniformly closed in order for a section to sound or feel closed, nor do all the elements need to be uniformly open for a section to sound or feel open. One variable (e.g., a symmetric phrase structure forming a fragmented section) may imply stopping, while another variable (e.g., the harmonic cadence is a half cadence) may imply movement. It is the mixing and matching of the many possibilities involved in combining the compositional variables that determine its exact effect on the form and ultimately on the listener.

The following comments that deal with the effect of a section of music ending open or closed must be understood in light of the previous paragraph. In other words, the following consists of generalities (the specifics of each individual song are full of subtleties) that you may find helpful as you grapple with the study of form.

---

[*] A simple example of an *AABA* chorus is found in Ex. 12.1.

verse/refrain   In a verse/refrain song, with the refrain in the end position, the verse remains open until the refrain closes the section. It is this closure that causes the listener to rightly hear a verse/refrain song as a one section song.

‖ verse—*open*   refrain—*closed* ‖

verse/chorus   Most verse/chorus songs have verses that end open and lead to the chorus.

‖ verse—*open* | chorus—*closed*   ‖

bridge sections   Most bridge sections end open. The *B* (bridge section) of an *AABA* song leads back to the last *A*.

‖ A | A | B—*open* | A   ‖

The transitional bridge of a verse/transitional bridge/chorus song leads to the chorus and, therefore, tends to be open.

‖ verse | transitional bridge—*open* | chorus   ‖

The primary bridge, found in verse/chorus songs, either leads back to a verse or, more usually, leads to the final chorus and, therefore, tends to be open.

‖: verse | chorus   :‖ primary bridge—*open* ‖ chorus   :‖

assignment   *Choose a song to study in depth. You will need a recording and sheet music or —better by far—transcribe the song in the form of a lead sheet.*
Ask yourself the following:
1. *Do I perceive the song in sections? If so, what is causing me to differentiate one section from another?*
2. *How closed or open is each section? What compositional variables are determining the effect?*
3. *If I do not hear the song in sections, what techniques have been employed to cause the song to retain interest, to retain coherence, to establish contrast?*

PART 2

Melody-Harmony
Relationships

Chapter 13

Functional Harmony and Harmonic Progession

Degrees of stability and tone tendencies remain the same, whether conceived horizontally (melodically) or vertically (harmonically).

Diamond notes are stable. Darkened noteheads designate the leading tone (most unstable) and the 4th degree of the scale, which is almost as unstable as the leading tone. Heightening the instability of these two notes is their tendency to resolve by a half-step (7–1; 4–3).

Ex.13.1

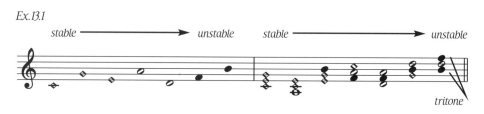

tonic function triads

The most stable chord in a key is the I chord because it contains all three stable tones.

Chords that contain two stable tones are next in the hierarchy: vi and iii. iii contains the unstable leading tone, thereby making it less stable than vi.

Ex.13.2

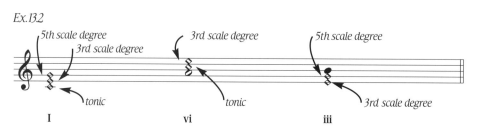

subdominant function triads

Less stable than any tonic function triad is the IV chord, which contains the 4th degree of the scale and has only one stable tone. Less stable than the IV chord is the ii chord, which contains the 4th degree of the scale and has no stable tones.

Ex.13.3

The vi chord can also function as a subdominant. In this capacity, it usually precedes the dominant harmony.

Ex.13.3 The vi Acting as Subdominant

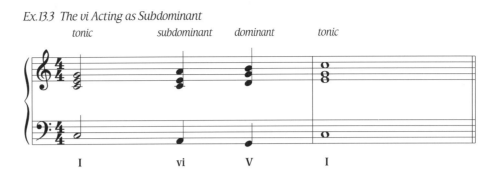

The vi is a chameleon-like chord, changing function according to its placement in the progression.

Ex.13.4b The vi Acting as Tonic

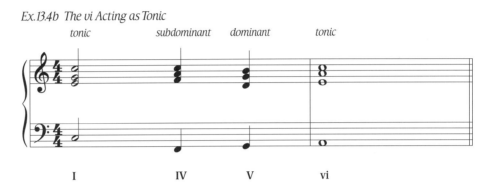

dominant function triads   Less stable than any subdominant function triad is the V chord. Although the V chord contains one stable tone, its kinetic character is established by the leading tone and the strong attraction of the perfect 5th, especially when in the bass, to move to the tonic.

The vii° chord is the most unstable triad found in the major key diatonic system, containing the two least stable tones, the leading tone, and the 4th scale degree, together forming the tritone, the most unstable interval.

Ex.13.5

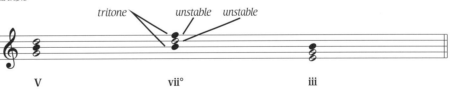

The iii chord is also chameleon-like and can serve as a dominant. In this capacity, it is most effective when its 3rd (the dominant of the tonality) is in the bass. (See Ex.13.6a and Ex.13.6b on the next page.)

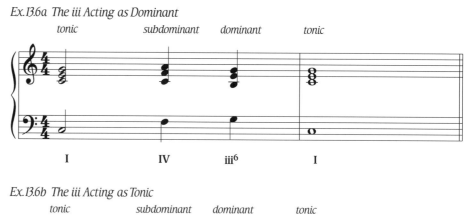

Ex.13.6a *The iii Acting as Dominant*

tonic   subdominant   dominant   tonic

I   IV   iii⁶   I

Ex.13.6b *The iii Acting as Tonic*

tonic   subdominant   dominant   tonic

I   IV   V   iii

stability/instability in harmonic progression

Harmonic progression is not radically different from melodic progression in as much as it results from the vertical coincidence of three (or more) melodies.

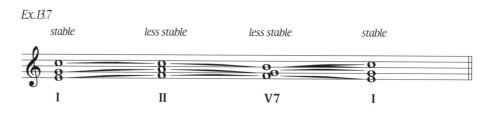

Ex.13.7

stable   less stable   less stable   stable

I   II   V7   I

A I–IV–V progression moves from a stable chord (I) to a less stable chord (IV) to the least stable chord (V). Obviously, this causes a directed movement (called a progression) to take place. If the progression then moves from the V chord to the I chord, a sense of stability occurs, giving us a point of rest or cadence.

functional harmonic progressions

The movement of harmonic stability to harmonic instability and vice versa in functional harmony is displayed in the following diagram:

Stability ⟶ *Instability*

Primary Tonic ⟶ Secondary Tonic

Tonic ⟶ Subdominant

Tonic ⟶ Dominant

Subdominant ⟶ Dominant

Diatonic ⟶ Chromatic

Instability ⟶ *Stability*

Chromatic ⟶ Diatonic

Dominant ⟶ Subdominant

Dominant ⟶ Tonic

Subdominant ⟶ Tonic

Secondary Tonic ⟶ Primary Tonic

In the analysis below, the arrow indicates the tonal movement either from a stable area to a less stable area or from a less stable area to a more stable area. The terms "stable" and "unstable" in this context are meant to show relative stability and instability of one chord to another within a progression.

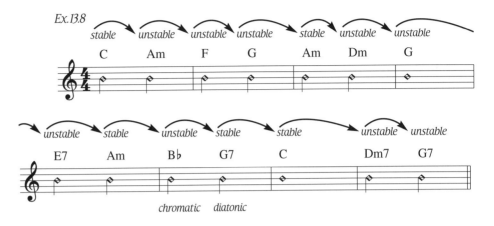

Note that the G7 in measure 6 is labeled "stable." This reflects the movement of the preceding chromatic ♭VII chord to the more stable diatonic dominant 7th.

exercise *Analyze the following progressions, designating their movement from stability to instability or from instability to stability.*

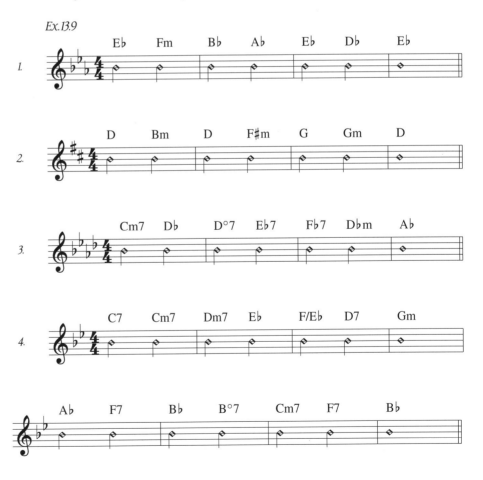

Chapter 14

A Unified Theory of Melody and Harmony

melodic progression   Any scale forms a hierarchical structure with its own tonal dynamics which, along with rhythm, control the progression of the music.

Ex.14.1

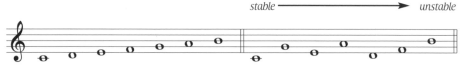

Hence, melodic progression can be analyzed.

Ex.14.2

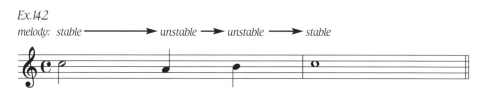

Here the progression is in one voice and is easily analyzed. When notes of a scale are verticalized (made into chords) the individual notes retain their place in the tonal hierarchy, but their combinations or mixtures cause so many gradations and subtleties that they practically boggle the mind. Hence, categorizing various groupings of chords into families of functionality helps us organize harmonies and perceive harmonic progression. (See Chapter 13: Melody-Harmony Relationships.)

When a melody is heard in conjunction with chords, the chord progression may coincide with the melodic progression.

Ex.14.3

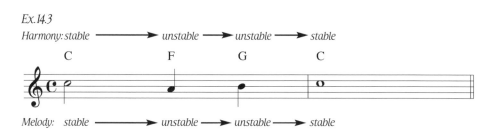

The chord progression may slightly alter our perception of the melodic progression.

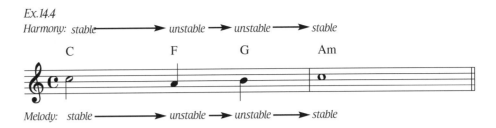

Ex.14.4

The chord progression may greatly alter our perception of the total music (the gestalt*).

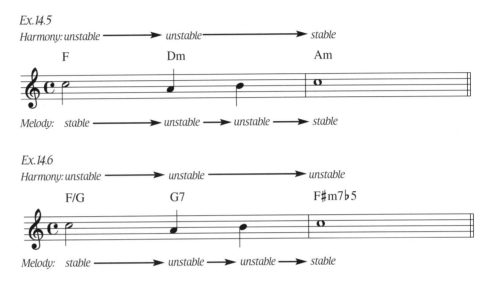

Ex.14.5

Ex.14.6

Because harmony plays such a strong role in our perception of the total music, one might assume that the progression in Ex.14.6 is from an unstable area to a more unstable area. But that analysis would not take into account the melody, which has begun on the tonic, the most stable tone, progressed away from it, and then returned.

An enormous perceptual change takes place in the following example:

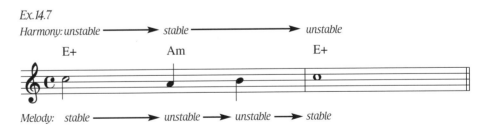

Ex.14.7

Here we have the tonal reversal of the melodic progression by the harmonic progression!

---

* A psychological or symbolic configuration so unified as a whole that its properties cannot be derived from its parts.

independent and dependent melodies

When considering melody/harmony relationships, there are a multitude of tonal choices. There are the moment-to-moment choices, where the consideration of the immediate note to the individual harmony is the focus, for instance, non-chord tones and the consonance/dissonance relationship of melody to bass. As important as these considerations are, they are not more important than the global aspect of tonality. Whether a melody is independent or dependent is a global consideration.

An *independent melody* is one with enough tonal interest and direction so it is not dependent on harmony to create musical interest. The appropriate harmony, of course, can enhance an independent melody, but the tonal interest of the melody is apparent even without the presence of harmony. Tonal interest is measured by the relationship of the melody to the tonal center (this is a global consideration).

"Yankee Doodle," "In My Life" by John Lennon and Paul McCartney, and "Over the Rainbow" by Harold Arlen and Yip Harburg are good examples of independent melodies.

Ex.14.8

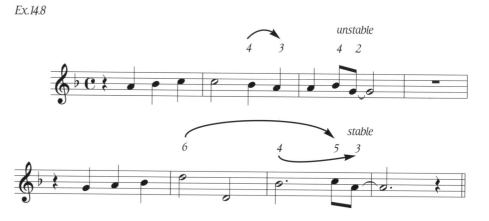

Ex.14.8 is an example of an independent melody. The unstable 2, which ends the first phrase, causes listener expectations to rise. Within the second phrase, more unstable tones appear which heighten listener expectations. In addition, a melodic step progression, D to C, and B♭ to A, gives the melody direction and a sense of forward motion.

A *dependent melody* is one which doesn't have enough intrinsic tonal interest and direction to sustain it and needs harmony (or possibly another voice, for instance, a counterpoint—often a guitar or bass riff) to create tonal interest. "One Note Samba" by Antonio Carlos Jobim, "For No One" by Lennon/McCartney and "'S Wonderful" by the Gershwin brothers and the verse section of "(I Can't Get No) Satisfaction" by Mick Jaggar and Keith Richards are examples of dependent melodies.

Consider the following melody. By itself, it is terribly drab; all its tones are stable and it ends on the tonic.

Ex.14.9

Choice harmonies certainly help create a phrase which has direction and some musical interest.

Ex.14.10

You may ask yourself, "Is it better to write an independent or a dependent melody?" Rather than ask that question, seek to understand what the total music needs in order to be interesting. We enter into the realm of the psychology of perception and musical memory when we wonder what is retained better, a dependent or an independent melody. In fact, many songs leave such a strong impression not only from their melody, but from the gestalt of melody, harmony and especially lyric, as well as instrumental texture and melodic fills, that it is impossible to pinpoint exactly what is being retained.

There is no doubt, however, that the question of musical interest, ("Is this interesting enough?") will occur to you over and over again as you attempt to create songs. In attempting to answer that question, a complete knowledge of the discrete values of each element of song as well as the various relationships between all of the elements of song is of utmost importance.

Examine the following melodies to discover how the interaction of melody and harmony affect your perception of the total music.

Ex.14.11

The melodic and harmonic progression parallel one another.

Ex.14.12a

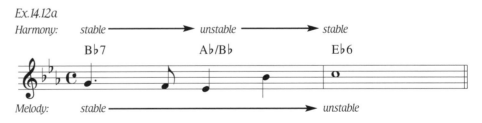

The melodic and harmonic progression contradict one another.

Ex.14.12b

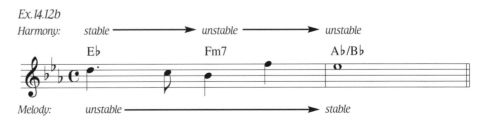

The melodic and harmonic progression contradict one another.

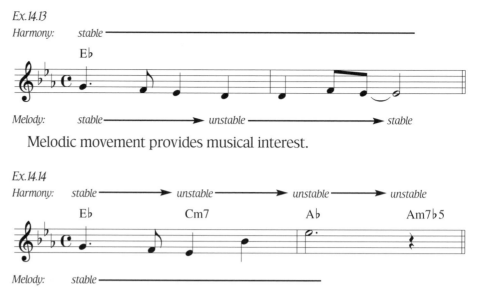

Ex.14.13

Melodic movement provides musical interest.

Ex.14.14

Harmonic movement produces musical interest.

why a unified theory?

In any given scale, the same tone tendencies and hierarchy exist whether tones are strung one after another as a melody or lined up vertically and struck together as a chord. This is what makes this theory a unified one. Your understanding and control of the total music can only come from your ability to separate melody from harmony, to examine its relationship to the outer tonality (the tonal center), and to be able to look at the stability/instability of both melody and harmony and then decide what is needed to make the total music work.

Simple tonal activity, with melodic and harmonic progression always tonally adjoined, produces one effect; complex tonal movement, such as when melody is fairly stable and harmony is fairly unstable, produces another effect. Myriad degress of effects can be created by mixing and blending basic tonal materials used in the making of popular songs. That is what makes this activity so fascinating!

assignment

The following melody begins stable and ends in an unstable area.

1. Write a chord progression for this melody that agrees with that tonal movement.

2. Now write a harmonic progression that contradicts the melody's tonal movement.

3. The following melody is composed of a majority of stable tones. Create a chord progression that provides forward motion to the music.

"Come Rain or Come Shine" The melody of this famous song is extremely dependent on its relationship to the harmony. The entire melody of this section is made up of stable tones in the key of F major. The melodic rhythm of the first four measures of "Come Rain or Come Shine" are repeated exactly in the next four measures, forming a symmetric section. This section is rhythmically closed. Since the last melody note of the section is also the tonic, the melodic pitch is also closed. However, the harmony at the final cadence of the section is a very potent dominant harmony built on the tonic, a I7 chord acting as a dominant of B♭, the subdominant in the key of F. This harmony effectively keeps the section open. In a sense, the rhythm acts as the boundaries of the section just as the walls of a room act as its boundaries. But the harmony, like an open door, is a beckoning invitation to enter another room.

As you study great songs, you will discover some hidden meanings that the marriage of words and music brings to light. Here, Harold Arlen's repeated notes evoke a Johnny Mercer lyric that focuses on ardent resolve and commitment ("I'm gonna love you like nobody's loved you"), while Arlen's harmonic acumen evokes Mercer's acknowledgment of life's everchanging nature ("come rain or come shine"). What amazes and transports us is how all of this information, both rational and emotional, takes place in the first four measures of the song.

Ex. 14.15

Come Rain or Come Shine

Lyrics by Johnny Mercer
Music by Harold Arlen

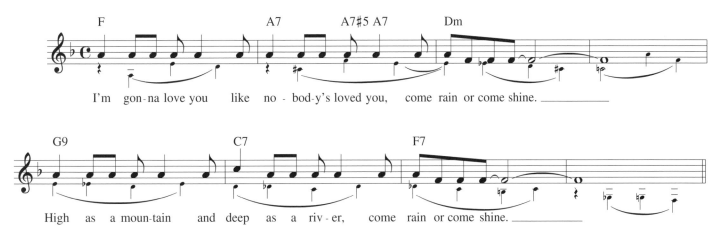

I'm gon-na love you like no-bod-y's loved you, come rain or come shine.

High as a moun-tain and deep as a riv-er, come rain or come shine.

Chapter 15

Non-Chord Tones and Tensions

non-chord tones

Non-chord tones are melody notes that are not found in the harmonic underpinning. They may appear both on the beat (accented) or between beats (unaccented). It is important to understand the kinetic nature of non-chord tones. When a melody note does not conform to the chord sounding with it, that melody note will create a dissonance that will usually seek resolution to a compatible harmony note. In other words, the usual activity of a non-chord tone is to resolve to a chord tone. This movement from dissonance to consonance, or tension to release, is one of the basic tenets of music. It produces interest and is one way to create melodic emphasis and/or melodic progression. Non-chord tones are more apparent and sound more dissonant (hence are more kinetic) when they appear on the beat. The following terms have already been encountered (Chapter 7). The new definitions refer to melody in relationship to chords, whereas the previous definitions referred to connectives or embellishments of structural melodic tones, without any reference to harmony.

1. **Neighbor Tone (NT; also known as an auxiliary)**—a non-chord tone that moves by step away from a chord tone and then returns to the same chord tone. There are two types of neighbor tones: upper and lower. A neighbor tone may either be unaccented or accented.

Ex.15.1

2. **Changing Tone (CT; also known as indirect resolution)**—two successive neighbor tones that surround the chord tone of resolution and resolve to it.

Ex.15.2

3. Passing Tone (PT)—a non-chord tone that moves by step between one chord tone and another chord tone in the same direction. A passing tone may either be unaccented or accented.

Ex. 15.3

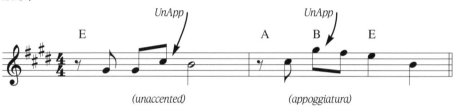

4. Unprepared Approach Tone (UnApp)—a non-chord tone that is approached by skip and resolves by step to a chord tone. An unprepared approach tone may be accented or unaccented. An accented UnApp is also commonly known as an *appoggiatura.*

Ex. 15.4

5. Escape Tone (ET)—a non-chord tone that moves by step from a chord tone but skips, usually in the opposite direction, to a chord tone. Escape tones usually appear on the weak part of the beat.

Ex. 15.5

6. Anticipation (Ant)—a non-chord tone that anticipates a tone of the next chord. Note: the term "anticipation" refers here to a tone that is sounded twice, first as a non-chord tone and then as a chord tone. This definition differs somewhat from the use of the term among arrangers, who use it to refer to a rhythmic anticipation causing a syncopation.

Ex. 15.6

7. Suspension (Sus)—a note that first appears as a chord tone (preparation), is sustained, becomes a non-chord tone on a new chord (suspension), and finally resolves to a chord tone (resolution).

Ex.15.7

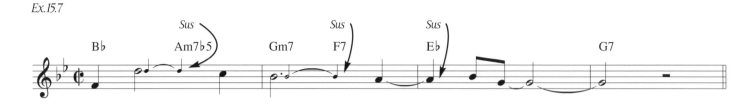

assignment *Write melodies to the given chord progressions incorporating the specific non-chord tones requested. Draw an arrow to each of the non-chord tones used, naming them (use abbreviations) as they occur.*

Ex.15.8 Use Accented PT, NT, Ant.

Ex.15.9 Use UnApp, both Accented and Unaccented.

Ex.15.10 Use PT, both Accented and Unaccented, and Sus.

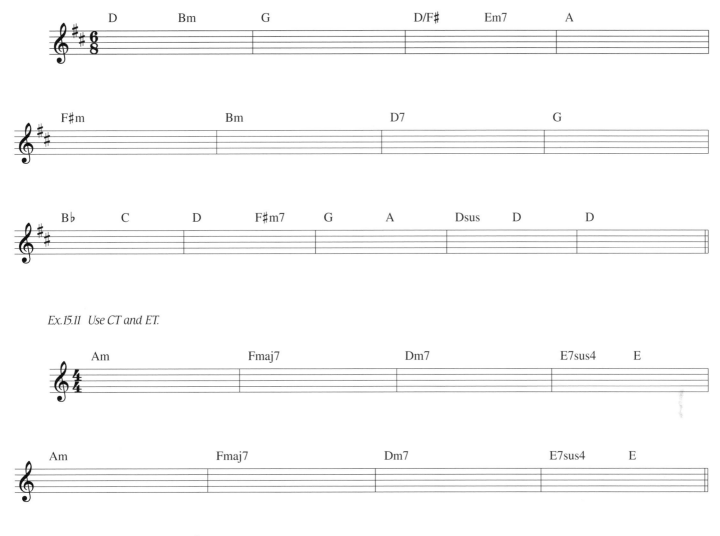

Ex.15.11 Use CT and ET.

assignment *Draw an arrow to each of the non-chord tones and, using abbreviations, name them.*

Ex.15.12

"Killing Me Softly" The entirety of this very popular song, including the chorus shown here, is full of non-chord tones. The non-chord tones found here are accented passing tones, unprepared approach tones or suspensions. Notice the melodic step progression found in the melodic outline that helps propel this melody from beginning to end.

More subtle, but very important, is the relationship of the melody, i.e., phrase, to the harmony, i.e., phrase. Notice that only in the first phrase do melody and harmony begin together. After phrase 1, the pickup notes—beginning on the third beat of measure 2—energize the phrase structure, first calling your attention to the beginning of the melodic phrase and then to the point in the phrase where the non-chord tone occurs on the new harmony.

Killing Me Softly

Words by Norman Gimbal
Music by Charles Fox

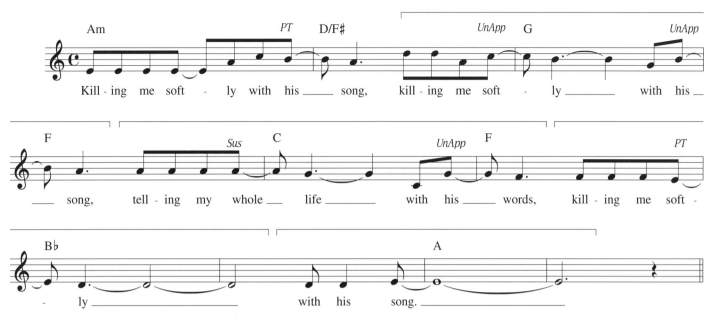

tensions   Certain popular music styles, especially jazz, R&B, and modally-based pop songs, allow for dissonant intervals from the root of the chord such as 9ths, 11ths, and 13ths to occur unresolved. These notes (called "tensions") may also be incorporated into the harmonic underpinning to create 9th, 11th, and 13th chords.

non-chord tones and tensions   Confusion can arise from the difference between the two terms: *non-chord tones* and *tensions*. This is due to the fact that both terms refer to what outwardly may look like the same musical configuration. The difference basically lies in the treatment of the configuration, the amount of rhythmic emphasis given to the note in question, and the total context (style) of the music.

In Ex.15.14, the F and D falling respectively on beats 1 and 2 are absorbed into the underlying harmony, rather than being emphasized by it. The non-chord tones E♭ and C appear on the upbeats and, therefore, do not call attention to themselves. They are *unaccented non-chord tones* (in this case, passing tones) that resolve by step to chord tones.

Ex.15.14

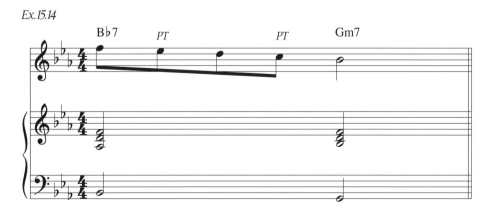

Unlike Ex.15.14, in Ex.15.15 the F and D, falling respectively on beats 1 and 2, are emphasized by the choice of harmonies. The dissonances are more pronounced because the non-chord tones appear on the beat. They are treated as *accented non-chord tones* (in this case, passing tones) and are, therefore, not incorporated into the harmonic underpinning.

Ex.15.15

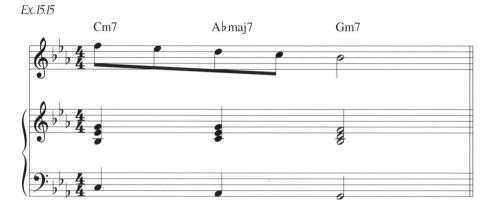

Ex.15.16 treats the F and the D as *tensions* and incorporates them into the harmonic underpinning. Incorporating these tones into the chords produces a harmonically richer context (a stylistic consideration).

Ex.15.16

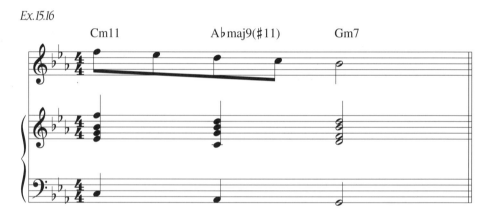

In the following example, the F in measure 1 and the D in measure 2 are accepted into a richer tonal context. These tones are considered *tensions* because of their melodic isolation and their strong rhythmic emphasis, whether or not they are purposely incorporated into the harmonic underpinning.

Ex.15.17

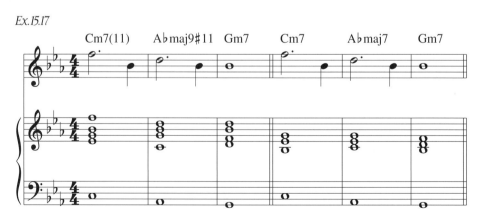

assignment *Draw an arrow to each of the melody notes that can be called a tension and name it (e.g., 9; b9; #9; 11; #11; 13; b13).*

writing tip The term *non-chord tones* sounds forbiddingly academic, but please do not dismiss this subject lightly. Understanding how to use non-chord tones in melody writing could make all the difference in your ability to compose an interesting melody. Consider the difference between the two phrases below:

Chapter 16

Making Harmonic Choices

harmonic choices

You may write a song beginning with any of four major areas: the lyric, the melody, the harmony, or the groove. No matter where you begin, the process sooner or later involves combining all four elements into a cohesive whole.

If you have composed the melody first or have written both lyric and melody, the next process will involve making harmonic choices. Although a definite order is given, the following activities are not usually done as singularly as outlined and, in fact, may be done in any order or simultaneously.

1. Choose a harmonic rhythm. The tempo and the breadth needed within the melodic phrase help determine where the chords are placed. Chords placed too closely together may crowd the melody, especially in moderate to fast tempos. On the other hand, if the rate of harmonic activity is too slow, there may not be enough musical interest to sustain the composition. The choices you initially make concerning harmonic rhythm should serve as a general outline, one which can and should be altered as more specific harmonies are decided upon.

Ex.16.1

2. Decide which notes within the phrase are to be chordal and which are to be non-chordal, and whether you are incorporating tensions both in the melody and in the harmony. A melody usually hints at harmonic possibilities. Look for chordal, especially triadic, outlines in the melody; tones longer than a beat tend to be chordal rather than non-chordal.

Ex.16.2

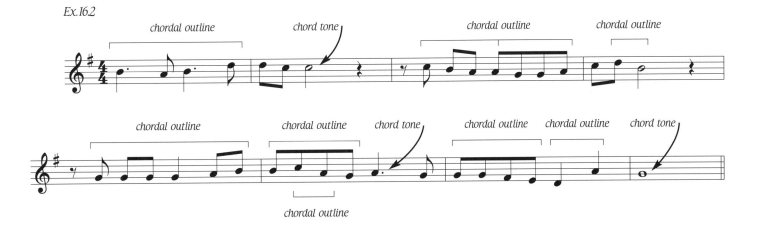

3. Group each metric division (each two beats, each measure, each four measures, etc.) according to harmonic function. Grouping according to harmonic function is a quick general way of deciding what your harmonies will be.

Ex.16.3

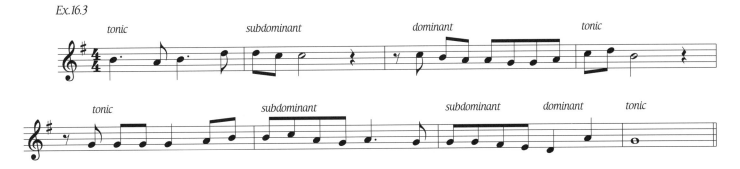

The melody in measure 1 could be harmonized using triads with any of the tonic function chords: G, E minor, or B minor. The melody in measure 2 could be harmonized by either of the two diatonic subdominant chords, C or A minor.

A melody note that is a chord tone has a great number of diatonic possibilities. It is either the root, 3rd, 5th, or 7th (or if tensions are incorporated, the 9th, 11th, or 13th) of a chord.

Ex.16.4

B, the main melody note of measure 1 could be:
the root of Bm
the 3rd of G
the 5th of Em
the maj7 of Cmaj7
the maj9 of Am7(add9)
the 11th of F#m7b5
the maj13 of D7(add13)

111

4. Study the melody, especially noting those areas in which harmony can be used to highlight the melodic design and movement. Look for "dead spots" in the melody, which are usually found after melodic cadences, on long notes, or during rests, where harmony can bridge the gap between two phrases or between two parts of the same phrase. If appropriate, add chords at these points.

The degree of melodic stability does not and should not always coincide with the same degree of harmonic stability. For example, the melody in measure 1 is mainly made up of stable tones and, therefore, implies a tonic harmony (stable). However, measure 1 could be harmonized with the less stable subdominant harmonies Cmaj7 or Am7.

Measure 6 presents an interesting problem. The first two beats outline either a tonic function or a subdominant function. If we want the harmony to highlight the B, then the B could be considered a non-chord tone (its dissonance to the chord helping to emphasize it).

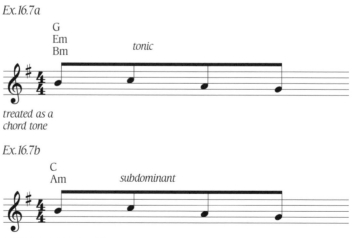

Study the following examples, which show three harmonizations of the same melody. In the first, the harmonic functions and the harmonic rhythms coincide with those originally outlined. In the second, different chords are chosen for the given harmonic functions (measure 5 does contain a change of harmonic function from tonic to subdominant) and the original harmonic rhythm is slightly altered. In the third, some of the original choices of harmonic functions are changed; chromatic chords and more elaborate harmonic rhythms are used.

assignment *Add chord symbols to the following melodies. Use two different sets of chord changes for each given melody. (You don't have to change each and every chord, but try to change as many as possible—especially changing harmonic function—while still retaining musical integrity.)*

114

Chapter 17

Melody/Bass Relationships

The relationship of the melody to the bass is extremely important because the bass
1. Provides the most prominent counterline to the melody.
2. Provides the greatest support for the melody of any harmonic voice.
3. Greatly affects the consonance or dissonance of the melody.

motion of the bass to the melody

The motion of the melody in relationship to the motion of the bass line is an important consideration. There are four types of motion possible between the melody and the bass:

1. **Oblique motion:** melody remains on the same note while the bass notes change or the bass remains on the same note and the melody notes change.

Ex. 17.1a Melody Remains on the Same Tone—Bass Moves

Ex. 17.1b Bass Remains on the Same Tone—Melody Moves

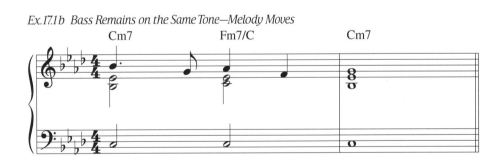

2. **Parallel motion:** bass and melody move by the same size interval in the same direction. Parallel motion between melody and bass line, especially in octaves or in perfect 5ths, can lead to monotony if continued for too many measures. It is an activity that negates one of the main purposes of harmony: to add, not simply duplicate, other voices.

Ex.17.2a Parallel Thirds between Bass and Soprano Melody

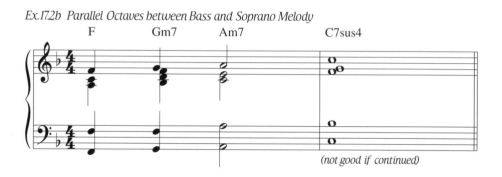

Ex.17.2b Parallel Octaves between Bass and Soprano Melody

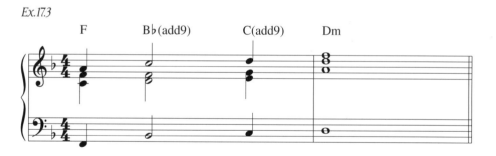

(not good if continued)

3. **Similar motion:** bass and melody move in the same direction (but not always in the same intervallic relationship).

Ex.17.3

4. **Contrary motion:** bass and melody move in opposite directions.

Ex.17.4a

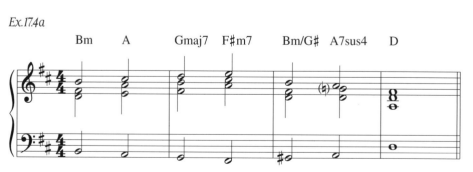

Another important consideration is the smoothness of the bass line itself. If the bass line has its own integrity, it will usually better support the melody and, as a bonus, will also furnish the song with another melodic line. If the roots of consecutive chords move by large leaps, the effect may be too disjunct. A smoother bass line may be achieved by inverting some of the chords.

Ex.17.4b

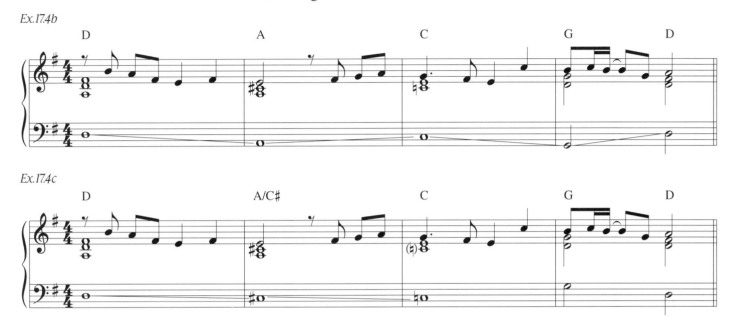

Ex.17.4c

chord inversions   The above example provides us with the first of four reasons to use an inversion of a chord: *to achieve a smoother bass line.*

If you want a chord to be less stable to itself, use an inversion. Inverting a chord (using a member of the harmony other than the root in the bass) makes the chord less stable to itself. A major or minor chord with the root in the bass is most stable to itself; in first inversion (with the 3rd in the bass) it is less stable to itself; in second inversion (with the 5th of the chord in the bass) it is even less stable to itself; and if a 7th chord has its 7th in the bass, it is least stable to itself. A major or minor chord is most stable to itself when in root position because its best interval, the perfect 5th, is not inverted (thereby coinciding with its position in the harmonic series). Diminished 7th chords and augmented triads do not contain a perfect 5th and are practically "rootless" because they are made up of equidistant intervals (in the case of diminished 7th chords: all minor 3rds; in the case of augmented triads: all major 3rds). Therefore, inverting them, while having some effect, has much less of an effect than inverting either a major or a minor chord (Ex.17.5a and 17.5b).

Ex.17.5a

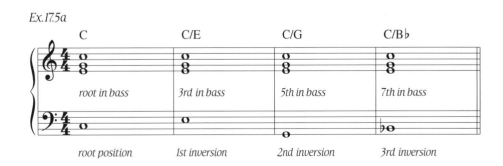

117

Ex.17.5b

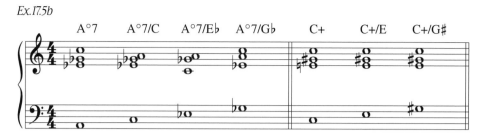

Examine the following example and notice how "flat-footed" the consecutive root position chords cause the music to sound.

Ex.17.6a

Now, examine the same melody and chords, but this time with some of the chords appearing as inversions. Notice how buoyant the music has become due to the use of inversions.

Ex.17.6b

Both renderings, however, have merit. Each points to a slightly different style: the first, possibly a rougher hewn one; the second, a slightly more sophisticated style.

Chord inversions are sometimes used to create a specific intervallic relationship between the bass and the melody, which affects the consonance or dissonance of the melody. In the following example, in order to retain the rich quality of the interval of the 3rd, which appears on the downbeat of measure 1, the D7 chord, which appears on the third beat of measure 1, is put into first inversion. If the D7 had been used in root position instead, the hollow sounding interval of the perfect 5th would have appeared between melody and bass and would have been less satisfying.

Ex.17.7

Country Ballad

Chord inversions are sometimes used to emphasize or change the harmonic function of a chord. Although a complete study of this subject is beyond the scope of this book, the following example should give you an idea of how chord inversions can affect harmonic functionality.

Ex. 17.8

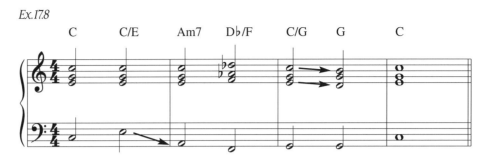

In measure 1, the 3rd of the I chord, E, leads beautifully down a 5th (a very strong root movement) to the root of the vi chord, the inversion helping to create a stronger bass motion from the I chord to the vi chord.

In measure 2, the ♭II chord in first inversion emphasizes its subdominant function (F, in the bass, is the subdominant of C major).

In measure 3, both the placement of the I chord within the total progression and its inversion (the second inversion, an inversion that greatly destabilizes the chord's relationship to itself) cause the I chord to sound like a V chord with a double suspension; in other words, the inversion has caused the I chord to function as a dominant!

Be warned that *the arbitrary use of inversions generally weakens a progression.* If you're going to use an inversion, try to make sure that it is a preferred choice over the same chord in root position or that it creates a better bass/melody relationship.

One additional bit of information that may help you understand how and when to use inversions: although putting a chord in an inversion will make it less stable to itself, it may make it more stable or less stable to the tonal center. In the next example (Ex. 17.9), the vi chord in first inversion causes it to be less stable to A, its own root, but much more stable to the key C major (the most stable tone in the key is now in the bass). Placing the E minor chord in first inversion makes it both less stable to itself and less stable to C, the tonal center. In first inversion (with the G in the bass), the inversion highlights the dominant function. The E minor chord in second inversion (placing the leading tone in the bass, thereby highlighting it) is both less stable to itself and less stable to C, the tonal center. Playing the example should expose the fact that the use of inversions has made the second chord in measure 1 little more than a slightly altered tonic chord (the vi chord with its 3rd in the bass) sounds like the

I chord with an added 6th), whereas in measure 2, the iii chord in both first and second inversions functions as a dominant (especially in first inversion, sounding like a G chord with an added 6th).

Ex.17.9

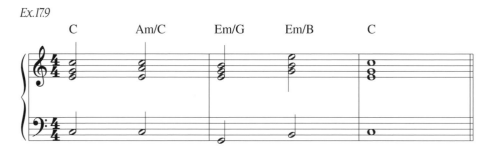

A common error is mistaking a change in chord position as a chord inversion. The position or voicing of a chord does not involve a change of bass note, whereas an *inversion of a chord always means that a chord tone other than the root is in the bass.*

Ex.17.10

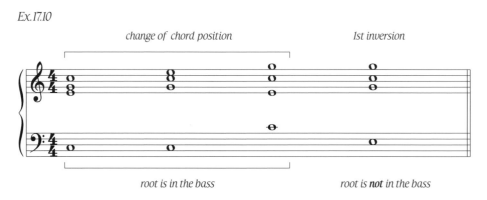

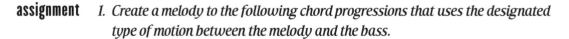

assignment *1. Create a melody to the following chord progressions that uses the designated type of motion between the melody and the bass.*

Ex.17.11 Similar Motion

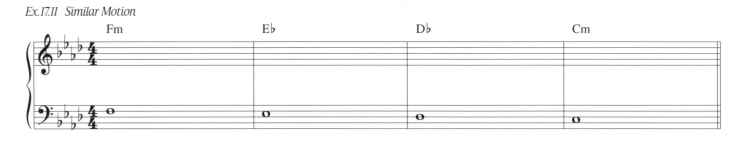

Ex.17.12 Contrary Motion

120

2. *Harmonize the following melodies using the designated type of motion between the melody and the bass. Notate the bass notes.*

Ex.17.13 Oblique Motion

Ex.17.14 Parallel Motion

3. *Retain the same chords, but invert some of them in order to enhance the total effect of the music.*

Ex.17.15

4. *Create an 8- to 16-measure section of a song (melody and chords). Use at least three of the chords in inversions, making sure to use the inversions in a purposeful way. (This part of the assignment is to be done on separate manuscript.)*

consonance/dissonance of intervals

You will find it very useful to know the relative consonance or dissonance of intervals. After all, the relationship of the melody to the bass is an interval. So is the relationship of the melody to the root of the chord (the chord may be in an inversion and its root may, therefore, not be in the bass). Further, the chord itself is made up of intervals. The following chart, which measures intervallic consonance/dissonance, groups intervals in a general way (called sets) that I have found very helpful. Set 1 is the most consonant; Set 2—a little more dissonant; Set 3—quite dissonant; and Set 4—the most dissonant. Keep in mind that this chart refers to diatonic intervals (intervals found in one key) since chromatic notes add another dimension of dissonance to the mix.

Ex.17.16 *Intervallic Consonance-Dissonance Chart*

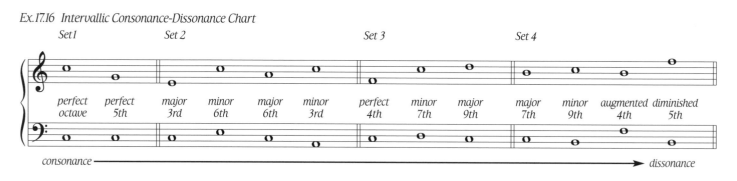

These intervals are all found in C major. I've tried to use the note "C" as often as possible in the intervals shown, but I must use other notes with the tritone in order to remain diatonic.

This chart is helpful in many instances, for example, in finding the right bass notes when a melody note repeats, in creating a real sense of progression from consonance to dissonance or vice versa, and in highlighting important melody notes.

In Ex.17.17a, "C," the most stable note in C major, is placed in the melody and set against bass notes, which increase in dissonance from Set 1 to Set 4.

Ex.17.17a

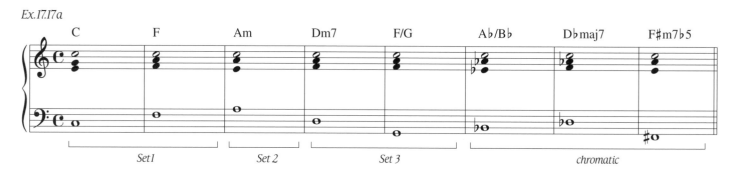

In Ex.17.17b, "B," the most unstable note in C major, is placed in the melody and set against bass notes, which grow in intervallic dissonance from Set 1 to Set 4. First play just the melody and bass notes; then play the inner voices, which give the sound of the entire chord. Notice that while the intervallic dissonance between the melody and bass increases, the tonal dissonance from the first chord to the last chord decreases. (There is a tonal movement in the key of C from instability to stability.)

Ex.17.17b

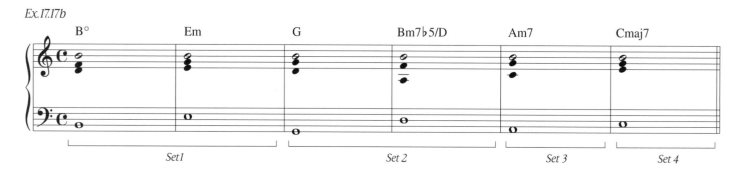

This last example leads to the conclusion that when harmonizing a melody, you must consider both the melody-to-bass note and melody-to-root note relationships, as well as the chord's functional relationship to the tonal center. Another example might make this more clear.

Consider the "B" in the following melody (again in C major):

Ex.17.18

In Ex.17.19, B°, Em (Set 1), and G and Bm7♭5/D (Set 2) all imply the dominant harmony, thereby agreeing with the instability of the melody note. Harmonic agreement does not add another dimension to the music or even necessarily highlight the dissonance of "B." The dissonance of "B" is highlighted, however, by the tonic chords Am7 (Set 3) and Cmaj7 (Set 4), which contrast to it and, by doing so, add another dimension to the music. The dissonance of "B" is heightened to an even greater degree by placing the F chord (Set 4) underneath it. Now the "B" is a tritone from the bass and is made to act as a non-chord tone, resolving to "C" on the fourth beat.

Ex.17.19

Now consider the final C, which tonally resolves the melody. Our harmonic choices could allow the listener to hear a full resolution: C (Set 1); a somewhat less than full resolution: C/E (Set 2) or a deceptive Am (Set 2); or to experience next to no resolution at all: F (Set 1), F/G, Dm7 (Set 3). Through an interesting choice of harmony, we might even consider making "C" seem to be more dissonant than the previous "B." F#m7b5 is a chromatic chord in C built on #4 that increases the tonal dissonance enough to make the end of the phrase its highest point of tension!

In making a choice, there is no right or wrong except in relationship to what precedes and what follows each musical event. Knowing the relationships of tones to the tonal center as well as the intervallic consonance/dissonance of the melody to the bass and to the root of the chord gives you the power to choose wisely and well as you mix these alchemical ingredients together to form your composition.

assignment   *1. Choose chords that give the following dependent melody a real sense of progression. Be especially sensitive to the intervallic dissonances between bass note and melody.*

Ex. 17.20

2. Find chords that highlight the melodic climax and then gradually move towards tonal stability.

Ex. 17.21

climax

124

Chapter 18

Harmony in Minor

There are distinct and important differences between traditional harmony in minor and modal harmony in minor. These differences, which involve different root movement, chord progressions, and cadences, are predicated on:

1. The makeup of the scales themselves.
2. The way they have been used in the past.

traditional harmony in minor

Traditional harmony in minor is based on functional harmony, in other words, tonic, subdominant, and dominant functions. The dominant function plays the main role in defining the way minor is treated in a traditional harmonic context, due particularly to the importance of the leading tone.

The following three minor scales are used in traditional harmony.

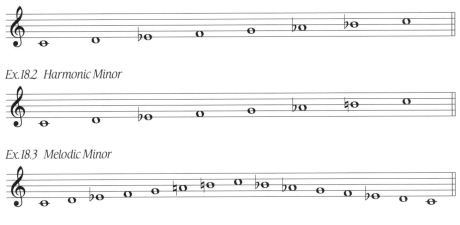

Ex.18.1 Natural Minor (or Aeolian Mode)

Ex.18.2 Harmonic Minor

Ex.18.3 Melodic Minor

The oldest of these scales, the natural minor, is a church mode named the *Aeolian mode.*

the harmonic minor scale

When the leading tone, in the course of history, began to dominate chord progressions and was used instead of the flat 7th scale degree, the harmonic minor resulted.

Ex.18.4 Characteristic Scale Degrees of Harmonic Minor

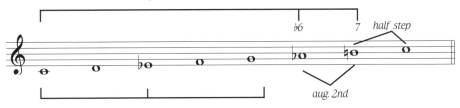

Harmonic minor is full of strongly kinetic tone tendencies. The scale has a leading tone, two tritones, and three unstable scale degrees that resolve to stable degrees by half-steps.

Ex.18.5 Stable to Unstable Scale Degrees of Harmonic Minor

Ex.18.6 Tone Tendencies of Harmonic Minor

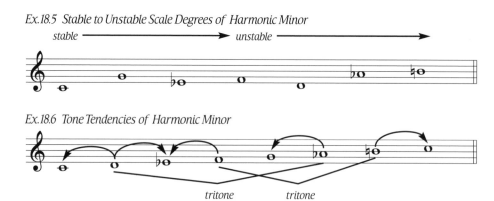

Ex.18.7 Diatonic Triads of Harmonic Minor

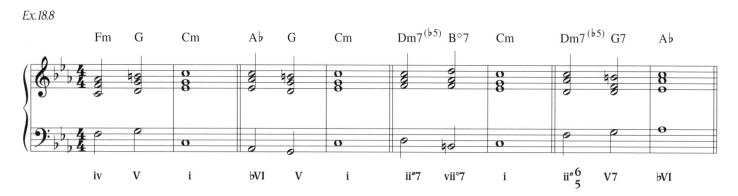

The group of triads and 7th chords produced by this scale has very strong cadencing possibilities.

Ex.18.8

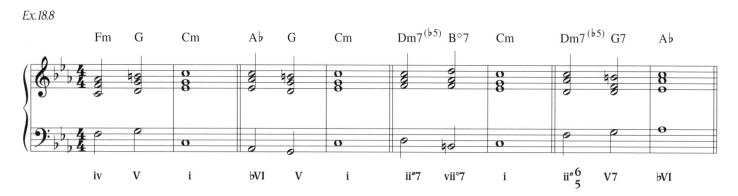

the melodic minor scale

The melodic minor scale in its ascending form resembles the *Dorian mode* (note the major 6th scale degree) with the leading tone replacing the flat 7th degree.

Ex.18.9 Dorian Mode

Ex.18.10 Melodic Minor Ascending

In the descending form, the Melodic Minor is the same as the natural minor scale.

Ex.18.11 Melodic Minor Descending

The harmonization of the melodic minor scale generates all the chords found in diatonic traditional minor and furnishes the composer with a colorful palette of new and usable chords.

Ex.18.12

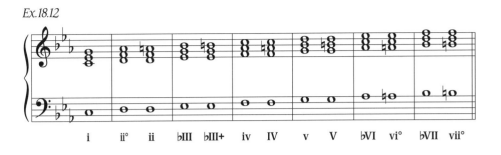

i   ii°   ii   bIII bIII+ iv   IV   v   V   bVI vi° bVII vii°

melody/harmony relationships in minor The minor scales are not usually treated as three separate scales but rather are combined in various ways into different facets of a single scale.

Ex.18.13

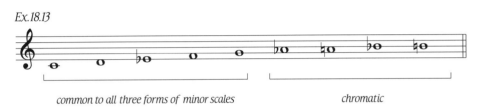

common to all three forms of minor scales   *chromatic*

A melody in one form of minor may be harmonized by chords of another form of minor. The natural minor melody in the following example appears with chords from the harmonic minor.

Ex.18.14

When composing a chord progression prior to the melody, consider
1. What scale or scales are implied by the harmony.
2. What other scales could work with the harmony.

Ex.18.15a Melodic Minor Ascending Implied by Harmony

Ex.18.15b Melody Consists of Scale Tones of the Melodic Minor Ascending

Ex.18.15c Melody Consists of Scale Tones of the Natural Minor

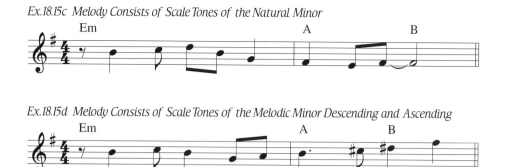

Ex.18.15d Melody Consists of Scale Tones of the Melodic Minor Descending and Ascending

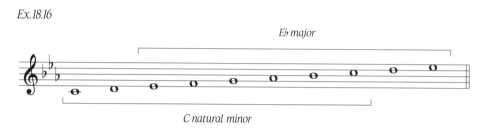

minor to major/major to minor

It is easy to move from a minor key to its relative major because of the following:

1. The notes of the natural minor and the notes of its relative major are the same.

Ex.18.16

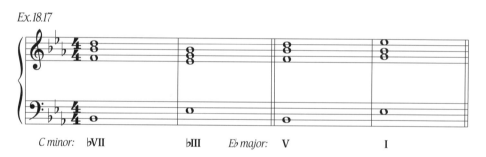

2. The progression ♭VII to ♭III in minor becomes V to I in its relative major.

Ex.18.17

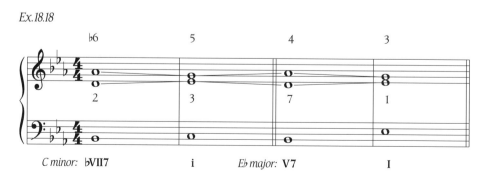

3. The tritone remains strategically placed both in a minor key and in its relative major. Unstable scale degrees 2 and ♭6 in minor resolve respectively to ♭3 and 5 (both stable scale degrees). In the relative major key, these same unstable tones become unstable scale degrees 4 and 7, which resolve to 3 and 1 (both stable tones).

Ex.18.18

use in form Minor keys are less stable than major keys; therefore, a movement from minor to major can be very satisfying. There are many compositions that begin in minor and end on a major chord. (The Picardy 3rd, common in Baroque music, is the raised or major 3rd of the tonic triad as the final chord in a work otherwise in minor.) I know of no compositions that begin in major and end in minor except for Vernon Duke's "Autumn in New York" and Harold Arlen's "Come Rain or Come Shine." The relationship of minor to major can be used in constructing the formal design of a song, which occurs in many verse/chorus songs where the verse is in minor and the chorus is in major.

Ex.18.19a

The opposite movement, from major to minor, is also useful in designing the formal structure of a song. This occurs most frequently in the *AABA* songs, where the *A* sections are in major and the *B* section is in minor. The return to the *A* section, which is in major, is a very satisfying move.

Ex.18.19b

In both minor-to-major and major-to-minor, the central lyric statement (title, hook) is likely to appear in the section that is in major.

The movement from minor to relative major or major to relative minor involves both a change in **modality**, e.g., A **minor** to C **major**, as well as a change in **tonality**, e.g., **A** minor to **C** major.

Ex.18.20

modal interchange   It is possible to change modality without changing the tonal center, e.g., A minor to A major. This is a move from minor to parallel major.

Ex. 18.21

This type of move occurs frequently within sections of songs but is rather infrequently used to differentiate one section from another. This is because a change of modality without a change of tonal center provides less of a contrast than one that changes both.

Borrowed chords from a parallel major or minor key, known as *modal interchange* chords, are simply considered expanded tonal vocabulary in the primary key. The following example in A major borrows both chords and melodic pitches from A minor:

Ex. 18.22

assignment   *1. Create a melody for each of the following chord progressions. Your melodic materials should consist of scales implied by the harmony as well as other minor scales that work well with the harmony.*

Ex. 18.23a

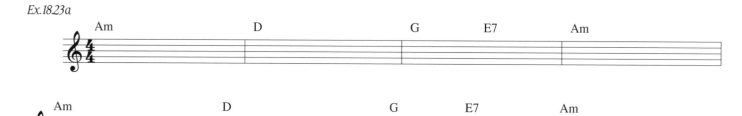

2. Create a chord progression (minimum length: eight measures) in minor that modulates to its relative major and then returns to the original minor key. Include a complete harmonic analysis of the progression. Compose a melody to it.

3. Create a chord progression (minimum length: eight measures) in major that uses chords found in the parallel minor. Include a complete harmonic analysis of the progression. Compose a melody to it.

4. Compose a verse/chorus song (melody and chords, lyrics optional) in two sections: the first section (the verse) in minor; the second section (the chorus) in major.

Chapter 19

Additional Melodic/ Harmonic Considerations

Harmony, by definition, involves a concerted sound, a sound that has an intrinsic weight, affecting the way we perceive both the meter and the phrase. The regular placements of chords can create a metrical pulse.

Ex.19.1

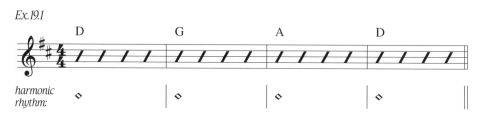

harmonic rhythm   Harmonic rhythm can coincide exactly with the meter,

Ex.19.2a

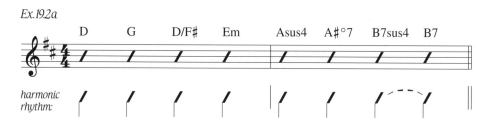

divide the meter into its usual strong subdivision,

Ex.19.2b

simply occur on downbeats,

Ex.19.2c

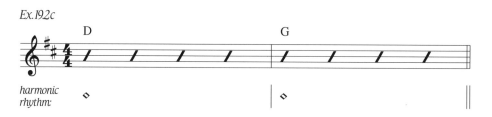

or even less frequently.

Ex.19.2d

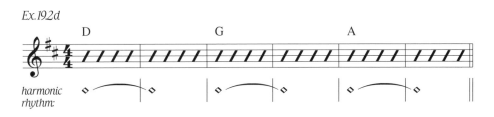

Generally, harmony changes more frequently in slower tempos. You can liken the harmonic underpinning of a composition to columns of a building supporting the structure. If you would like to move about in the building with freedom, a certain amount of space free of columns would have to be provided. Likewise, you achieve breadth within a musical phrase by allowing enough space between harmonic changes.

Harmonic rhythm, once established, tends to remain fairly constant. It is, however, sometimes a good idea to vary it, especially as a contrasting device between different sections of a song. Many verse/chorus songs harmonically decelerate in the chorus.

You should also consider the effect of harmonic change on the lyric. Since any change of harmony causes a stress to occur, this function can work toward—or against—the intended meaning of the phrase.

Both of the harmonic settings for the lyric are correct (the context of this particular line would be the deciding factor in determining exactly how correct), but note how the harmonic weight and tonal implications color each of the settings.

harmonic cadence The term *cadence* refers to a musical punctuation. A harmonic cadence refers to a succession of chords, especially to the last two chords that punctuate a section of music. There are four types of cadences. The *authentic cadence*, V (V7) to I, and the *plagal cadence*, IV to I, are called *full cadences* because they signify cadences that are harmonically closed.

Ex. 19.4 Authentic Cadence

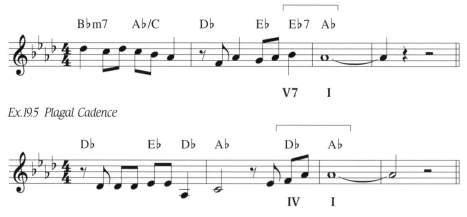

Ex. 19.5 Plagal Cadence

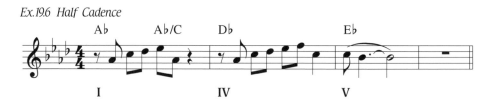

The *half cadence*, which usually ends on the V or an equally unstable chord, is harmonically open.

Ex. 19.6 Half Cadence

The *deceptive cadence*, which is usually V to vi or V to ♭VI, but may also be V to any chord that contains the tonic note, is half open (since it doesn't end on the tonic chord) and half closed (because the tonic note is in the melody.)

Ex. 19.7a Deceptive Cadence

Ex. 19.7b

Ex. 19.7c

134

use in form   Various sections within song forms usually call forth typical cadential patterns. For instance, a verse ending with a refrain will usually cadence on a tonic chord, thereby, harmonically closing it. A verse leading to a chorus will typically use a half cadence; a bridge *(B)* section of an *AABA* song would most likely use a half cadence to lead back to the last *A*. There are no firm rules constituting what type of cadence belongs where, but keep in mind that functionally, verse structures and bridge structures lead to other sections and tend to remain harmonically open while refrains and choruses usually end song systems and, therefore, tend to close.

harmony's effect on the phrase   Any numerical grouping with equal parts, whether it is a rhythmic grouping, a metric grouping, or the groups of measures in a phrase, yields the same pattern of accentuation. Harmony, by its metric placement, can affect the way we perceive the number of accents within a phrase and, thereby, the phrasal subdivisions. For example, the first measure of a two-measure phrase is strong, and the second measure is weak.

Ex.19.8a

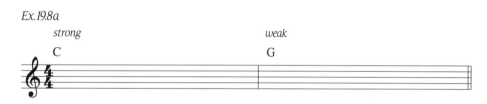

If, however, the harmonic rhythm within that two-measure phrase establishes a subdivision of the measure into four equal parts, a strong/weak/medium-strong/weak pattern of accentuation results.

Ex.19.8b

The areas of the harmonic phrase that call attention to themselves are the beginning of the phrase and the ending of the phrase. It is, therefore, important to be especially aware of the stability or instability of the harmonies chosen in these two areas.

Each harmonic phrase in the following country song is four measures long. The first and third measures of each phrase, since they are the strong measures, receive the most attention.

Ex.19.9

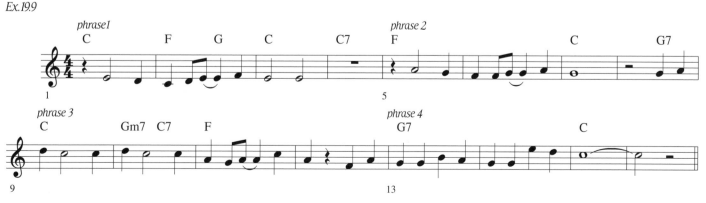

If we bypass the chords that come between and after the chords falling on the first and third measures of each phrase, we achieve the following analysis:

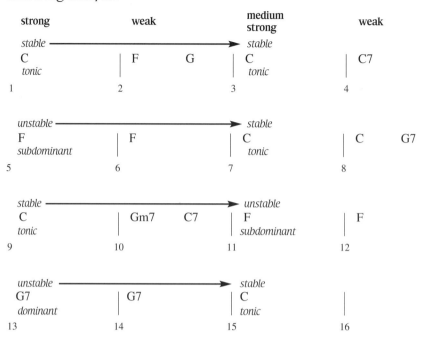

Notice that when the harmonic phrase reaches the tonic chord in the third measure of phrase 1, there is a need to create forward motion. This is accomplished in the fourth measure by the V7/IV, an unstable chromatic chord. Phrase 2 begins on the subdominant and again reaches stability in measure 7 on the tonic chord. The dominant 7th placed on the third beat of measure 8 supplies just enough energy so that the music doesn't totally succumb.

The third harmonic phrase begins on the tonic (measure 9) but quickly moves to two chromatic chords (measure 10) and then to the subdominant (measures 11–12), which feels like a place of resolution or rest. In reality, the subdominant is stable in relationship to the preceding chromatic chords but is unstable in relationship to the tonic. The fourth phrase begins on the unstable dominant, which finds resolution on the tonic (measure 15), and the section ends.

the harmonic-metric phrase and the melodic-rhythmic phrase

The melody occupying this harmonic progression mainly conforms to the dictates of the harmonic phrase. There are, however, important subtle differences in the phrase structure. As we have noted previously, harmony is usually aligned with meter and thereby creates the metric phrase. The melody is rhythmically and actively moving within and sometimes outside of the harmonic-metric phrase. Melody creates the rhythmic phrase.

Ex. 19.10

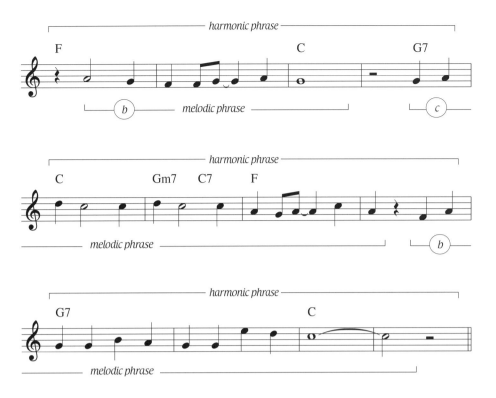

Some of the differences in the harmonic-metric phrase and the melodic-rhythmic phrase are apparent from the beginning. The harmony states the first beat of phrase 1, while the melody enters on the second beat, "pushing off" from the harmonic weight of the downbeat. The harmonic motion stops on the downbeat of measure 3, while the melody continues its activity, sounding a rhythm on the third beat of the third measure. While the melody rests on the fourth measure, the harmony (a secondary dominant, V7/V) creates movement and interest. In other words, *the melodic phrase coexists but doesn't always coincide with the harmonic phrase. Rather, it has a symbiotic relationship with it.*

Harmonically, both the first phrase and the second phrase—which serves to balance the first phrase—close on the tonic chord. This amount of harmonic-metric closure can be offset by a melody whose rhythmic phrase structure does not coincide with it. The rhythmic phrase structure of the melody is *abcb*. This melodic structure avoids the possible pitfall implied in the harmonic closure in the second phrase. An *aabb* or an *aabc* phrase structure would have been problematic with the given harmonic structure because it would have produced rhythmic closure while tonal closure was also occurring.

This bi-dimensional aspect of phrase structure is extremely important, for if the melodic-rhythmic phrase always coincided with the harmonic-metric phrase, as it does in my rewrite of Ex. 19.10, the resulting music would be unqualifyingly dull. (See the next page.)

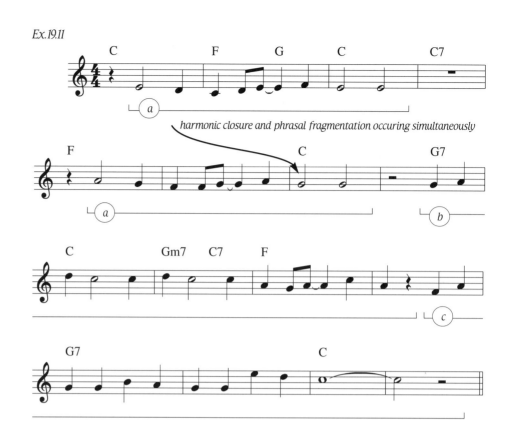

Ex.19.11

harmonic closure and phrasal fragmentation occuring simultaneously

assignment   *1a.   Supply chords that occur only on downbeats.*

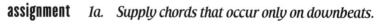

Ex.19.12a

Up tempo

1b.   Supply chords that occur every two beats.

Ex.19.12b

Moderately

2a.   Supply chords that occur on every beat.

Ex.19.13a

Ballad

2b.   Supply chords that occur once or twice per measure.

Ex.19.13b

Moderately

3. *Rewrite the harmonic cadence to avoid having both a melodic and harmonic closure occur simultaneously.*

Ex.19.14a

Ex.19.14b

4. *Rewrite the last melodic phrase to avoid having both a melodic and harmonic closure occur simultaneously. Supply chord(s) where indicated to give the music an additional push forward.*

Ex.19.15

"The Long and Winding Road" Lennon and McCartney's great understanding of wedding words perfectly to music accounts for the durability of many of their songs. "The Long and Winding Road" is a fine example of prosody at its deepest.

The 6th scale degree (6) is such a mildly unstable tone that it can almost substitute for the tonic, but it cannot replace it. In "The Long and Winding Road," Paul McCartney ends all but one phrase in the *A* section on it, where it gets "stuck" for some time, creating the song's iridescent prosody ("It always leads me here"). Eventually, 6 acts as a stepping stone to 7, which finally finds its way back to 1, as the lyric resonates to this event with "Lead me to your door."

The harmony is also elusive for some time. Notice how the tonic chord in measure 3 isn't given a chance to settle and instead acts as the dominant of A♭, the subdominant. Only in the final measure of this section is the tonic heard as a point of rest.

One other important function of harmony—that of either connecting or separating phrases—occurs in this song. In measure 5, a new melodic phrase begins; the harmony (A♭) from the previous phrase, however does not change, acting instead to effectively connect the two disparate phrases. This allows the lyric to continue ("The long and winding road that leads to your door will never disappear") and allows the listener to hear the first six measures of the song as one unit.

Ex. 19.16

The Long and Winding Road

Words and Music by
John Lennon and Paul McCartney

Chapter 20

Starting with a Chord Progression

Many songs are created by starting with a chord progression. This is a valid way to begin composing a song. A chord progression immediately provides a songwriter with an organizational tool—a number of measures grouped together tonally.

A chord progression could be simply a repetitious pattern, for example, consisting of two chords, one per measure, which repeat for 8, 12, 16, or more measures.

Ex. 20.1

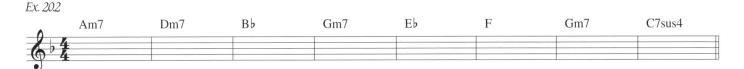

You may wish to write a chord progression that does not repeat.

Ex. 20.2

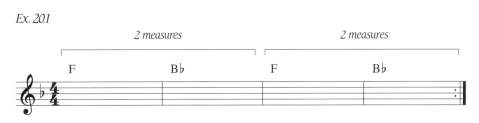

melodic integrity

Whatever type of progression you choose, the melody written to it should have its own integrity and not simply be dragged from place to place by the harmony. A number of factors help ensure melodic interest and integrity:

1. The melody could contain notes not found in the chords (non-chord tones, tensions).

Ex. 20.3a

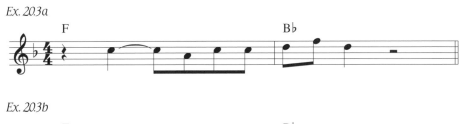

Ex. 20.3b

The melodies in Ex. 20.3a and 20.3b have exactly the same rhythm and melodic contour. There is little doubt that the melody in Ex. 20.3b is a more interesting melody because of the non-chord tones employed.

141

2. The melody could create different points of interest and areas of metric emphasis other than those of the harmonic phrase.

Ex. 20.4

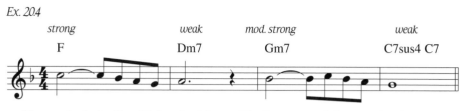

The melody in Ex. 20.4 coincides with the stress inherent in the harmonic phrase.

Ex. 20.5

The melody in Ex. 20.5 has rhythmic activity in the areas of weak harmonic/metric stress. This helps propel the music forward. It also creates a type of give-and-take activity between the harmonic and melodic phrases that continually enlivens the music. By comparison, the melody in Ex. 20.4 is rather lifeless.

3. The melody can begin and end in areas that differ from the beginning and ending of the harmonic phrase. The melody could even overlap two harmonic phrases. This technique is called *interlocking.* (Interlocking can be thought of as a particular type of elision.)

If you were to play the chord progression alone (Ex. 20.6), you would conclude that the harmonic progression is made up of two four-measure phrases.

Ex. 20.6

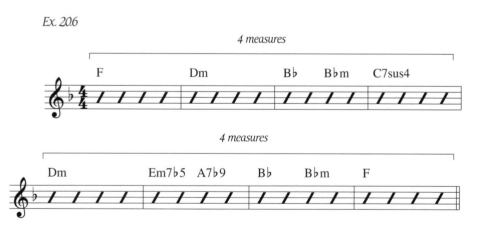

The melody composed to the same chord progression does not follow this phrase structure. The melody begun in measure 3 does not cadence in measure 4, but instead cadences on measure 5, the beginning of the new harmonic phrase!

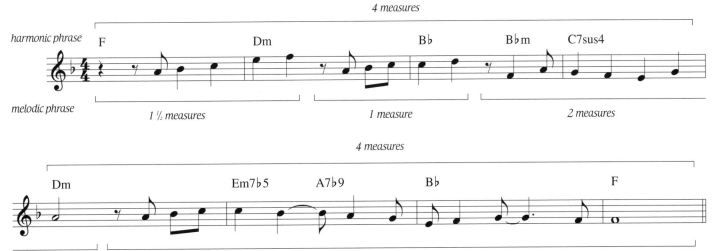

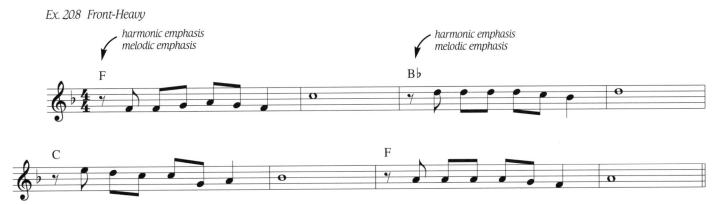

front-heavy melodic phrases; back-heavy melodic phrases

If a melodic phrase begins on a strong measure within a harmonic/metric framework, it is called a *front-heavy* phrase. Usually, in front-heavy phrases, the harmonic and the melodic phrase will coincide and, therefore, will be heard as one.

Ex. 20.8 Front-Heavy

If a melodic phrase begins on a weak measure within a harmonic/metric framework, it is called a *back-heavy* phrase. Beginning a melody on a weak measure creates an emphasis on that metric area. This causes a discrepancy in emphasis between the melodic phrase and the harmonic phrase, creating a "give and take" between them, which can propel the music in an interesting way. In general, back-heavy phrases tend to set up more expectations and create more forward motion than do front-heavy phrases.

Ex. 20.9 Back-Heavy

Compare Ex. 20.8 and Ex. 20.9. Notice that although the same rhythms and the same harmonic progression are used in both examples, Ex. 20.8, using front-heavy phrases, has only one point of emphasis, causing the music to be more monotonous. Ex. 20.9, using back-heavy phrases, has two points of emphasis: one created by melodic motion and the other created by harmonic weight and harmonic change.

Knowing that a melodic phrase and a harmonic phrase can coexist but not coincide is important, especially when using a short repetitious chord pattern (e.g., two or four measures in length). Using this technique furnishes the songwriter with one more way to create listener interest while retaining a simple vocabulary for each of the musical elements. (Interest results when simple elements are combined, producing a complexity of activity not readily apparent to the listener.)

Ex. 20.10

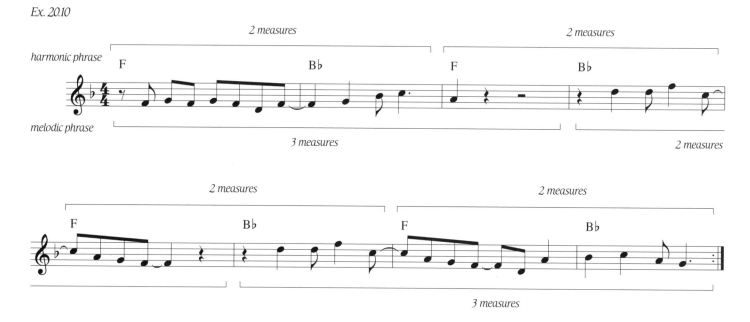

Ex. 20.10 is an eight-measure progression consisting of a two-measure harmonic phrase that repeats. The melody written to this fragmented harmonic progression consists of a three-measure front-heavy phrase, followed by a two-measure back-heavy phrase, followed by a three-measure back-heavy phrase.

For a good example of melodic phrase structure which retains its independence from the harmonic phrase structure, see Ex. 15.13, "Killing Me Softly."

assignment

1. *Create an 8- to 16-measure section of a song by starting with a non-repetitive chord progression. Compose a melody that retains its integrity by use of non-chord tones and/or tensions.*

2. *Create an 8- to 16-measure section of a song by starting with a 2- or 4-measure harmonic phrase that repeats. Compose a melody to the chord progression in which some of the melodic phrases are back-heavy phrases (i.e., that begin on weak measures within the harmonic-metric framework). Label the back-heavy phrases.*

Chapter 21

Pedal Point, Sus Chords, and Chords without Thirds

pedal point A *pedal point,* or more simply a *pedal,* is a note that is either sustained or repeated often enough to be heard as the primary note in a figure. It may occur in any part of the texture but is most often heard in the bass where it has the greatest effect on the tonal structure. Pedal points in the bass are most frequently found on the 1st (tonic) and 5th (dominant) degrees of the scale.

Pedal points can be very effective for a number of reasons. Notice the various functions the pedal point serves in the following example:

1. *To retain a basic tonal function by providing a tonal anchor.*
   The tonic D pedal point provides a tonal anchor for the first eight measures.

2. *To create harmonic interest.*
   The chord progression occurring above the pedal point causes dissonances against it that are tonally interesting. The chord progression in the first eight measures is quite ordinary by itself but is more interesting against the tonic pedal.

3. *To create more than one level of harmonic rhythm and harmonic function.*
   The harmonic rhythm is both eight measures (tonic pedal) and simultaneously one or two chords per measure. An entire chord progression, inclusive of all functions, exists in measures 1–8, and yet the entire progression is subservient to the tonic function because of the pedal point.

4. *To influence the form of a song by tonally sectionalizing it.*
   The tonic pedal point sectionalizes the first eight measures of the song.

5. *To allow for a greater freedom of melodic choice due to an expanded harmonic framework.*
   Certain notes in the melody, which would be suspect or avoided entirely if the tonic pedal were not present, for instance, the D in measure 6, are perfectly acceptable because of the presence of the tonic pedal.

The bass in the first eight measures of Ex. 21.1 is an *ostinato* (a figure persistently repeated throughout a composition or section). The tonic note, D, is the main structural tone of the ostinato and acts as a pedal.

Ex. 21.1

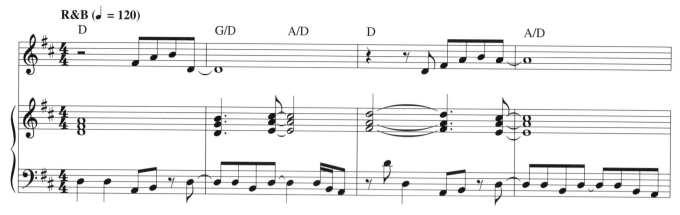

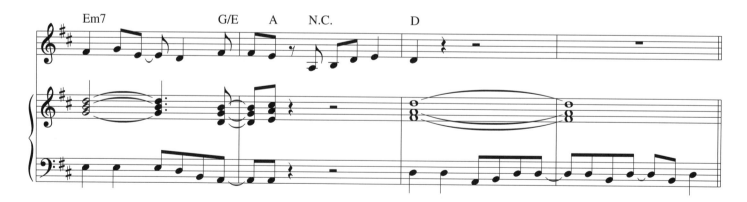

assignment   *Compose a 16-measure section of music (melody and chords) that uses a dominant pedal point for measures 1–8 and uses a tonic pedal point for measures 9–16. If a specific bass part is required, notate it; otherwise, use a lead sheet format.*

sus chords and chords without thirds

Sus chords and chords without thirds are part of present-day song vocabulary. These structures provide a certain amount of ambiguity to the harmony. This can be very useful to us because so much of what we do as songwriters is an attempt to avoid the obvious.

A sus chord is a chord in which the 3rd is omitted and is replaced by the note a perfect 4th above the root of the chord.

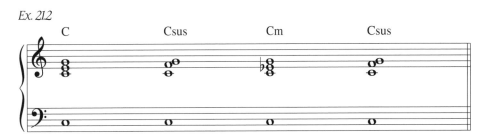

Ex. 21.2

Notice that without the 3rd, it is impossible to differentiate major from minor.

In most traditional music, the 4th above the root of the chord invariably resolves to the 3rd. This is still a viable option. In contemporary popular music, the sus4 just as frequently does not resolve to the 3rd.

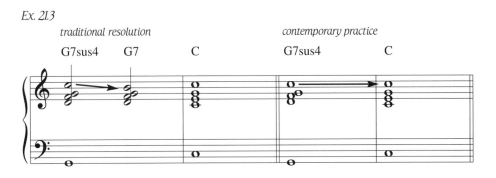

Ex. 21.3

More than one note in a chord may be suspended.

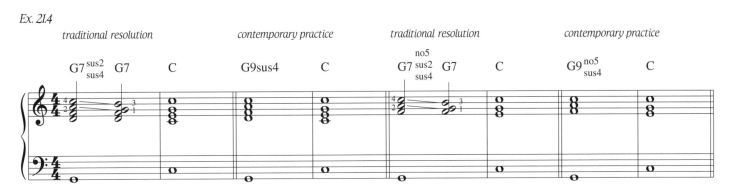

Ex. 21.4

The above structures translate into rather cumbersome chord symbols.

Easier-to-read symbols, consisting of a triad or 7th chord above a bass note, are commonly used. Unfortunately, these symbols do not indicate functional components of the chord.

Ex. 21.5

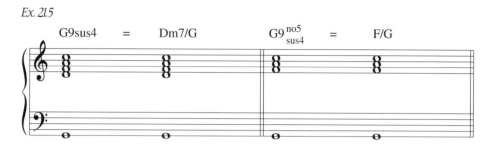

The function of a sus chord depends on its tonal setting.

Ex. 21.6

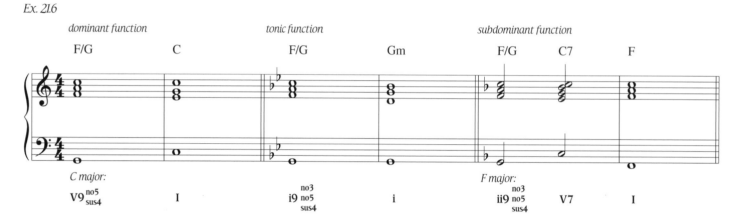

A quick way to create the above structure is, first, choose the root of the chord (G is the root); then build a major triad one step below the root (the major triad one step below G is F); and, last, place the triad above the root (placing the F triad over G produces F/G). This structure does not contain the 5th of the chord.

If you want the fuller sound that the inclusion of the 5th provides, the symbol is Dm7/G (root, 5th, 7th, 9th, sus4) or Dm/G, which contains the root, 5th, 7th, and 9th but does not contain the sus4. A quick way to create these structures is, first, choose the root of the chord (G is the root); then build a minor 7th chord or minor triad on the perfect 5th above the root (the minor 7th chord a perfect 5th above G is Dm7, and the minor triad is Dm); and, last, place the minor 7th chord or minor triad above the root (placing the Dm7 chord over G produces Dm7/G, and placing the Dm triad over G produces Dm/G).

Ex. 21.7

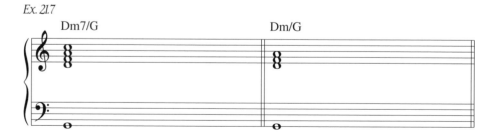

Minor key or modal interchange sus chords produce very interesting structures.

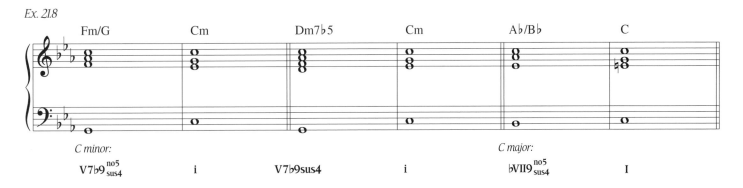

Ex. 21.8

| Fm/G | Cm | Dm7♭5 | Cm | A♭/B♭ | C |

C minor:

V7♭9$^{no5}_{sus4}$ i   V7♭9sus4   i

C major:

♭VII9$^{no5}_{sus4}$ I

chords without thirds   Some chords without thirds have evolved from pedal point formations. For example, when the V chord is placed above a tonic pedal, the following structure results:

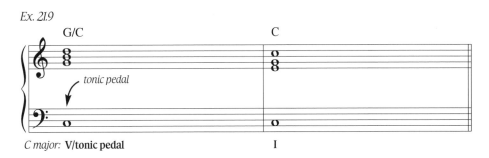

Ex. 21.9

G/C   C

tonic pedal

C major: **V/tonic pedal**   I

Placing the I chord over a subdominant pedal produces the following structure:

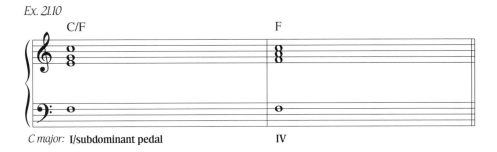

Ex. 21.10

C/F   F

C major: **I/subdominant pedal**   IV

Often, in contemporary songs, these structures appear without an ongoing pedal point.

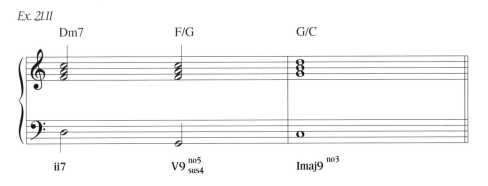

Ex. 21.11

Dm7   F/G   G/C

ii7   V9$^{no5}_{sus4}$ Imaj9^{no3}

149

Ex. 21.12

A quick way to create the above structure is, first, choose the root (C is the root); then build a major triad on the perfect 5th above the root (G is the triad); and, last, place that triad above the root (placing G above C yields G/C).

A common musical gesture, often used as an accompanimental device, results from moving back and forth from a chord without a third or a sus chord to a chord of resolution.

Ex. 21.13

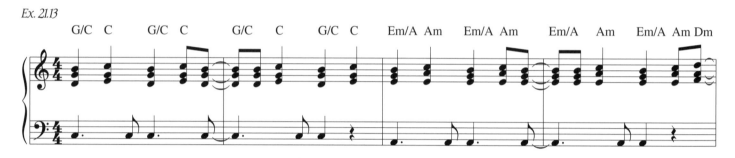

A common chord progression can be transformed by the use of sus chords. Here is a progression without sus chords and chords without 3rds.

Ex. 21.14

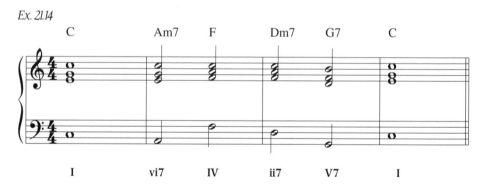

Here is the same progression, using sus chords and chords without 3rds.

Ex. 21.15

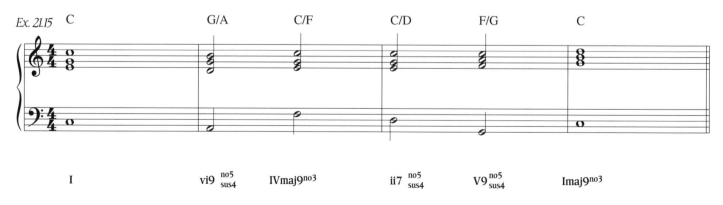

Differentiating between sus chords, chords without 3rds, and chord inversions can sometimes be problematic for students. If a chord can be built in 3rds and its root is not in the bass, it is an inversion.

Ex. 21.16

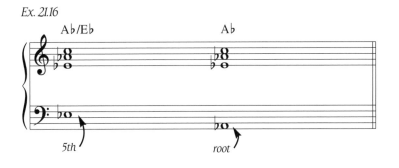

There are two exceptions to this rule:
1. A chord with the 5th in the bass (acoustically a very unstable inversion of a triad) may sometimes resolve to the following chord built on the same bass note. Although the first chord in Ex. 21.17 is called Eb/Bb, it functions as a Bb triad with a double suspension in it: 6–5, 4–3, and acts as a dominant.

Ex. 21.17

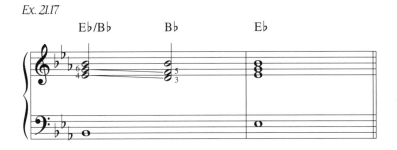

2. A chord that initially looks like a 7th chord, with the 7th in the bass, may be a sus chord with three notes suspended.

Ex. 21.18a The Normal Resolution of a Dominant 7th Chord with the 7th in the Bass

Ex. 21.18b Ab Triad with a Triple Suspension: 6–5, 4–3, 2–1

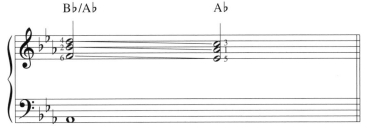

If a chord cannot be built in thirds, then it is probably a sus chord, a chord without the 3rd, or a chord over a pedal point. (A 9th, 11th, or 13th in the bass is extremely unlikely because these tones in the bass are acoustically unjustifiable.)

Ex. 21.19 This chord is a Bb9sus^{no5} chord, not an Ab(add9) with the 9th in the bass.

assignment   *1. Analyze the following chords in the given keys.*

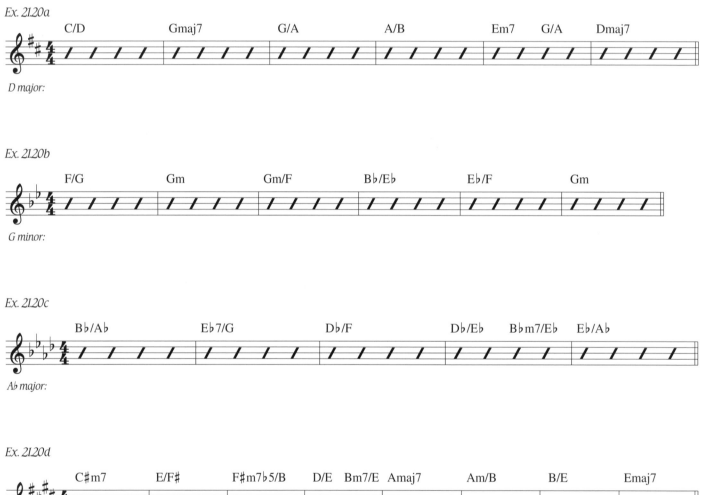

Ex. 21.20a

C/D   Gmaj7   G/A   A/B   Em7   G/A   Dmaj7

D major:

Ex. 21.20b

F/G   Gm   Gm/F   Bb/Eb   Eb/F   Gm

G minor:

Ex. 21.20c

Bb/Ab   Eb7/G   Db/F   Db/Eb   Bbm7/Eb   Eb/Ab

Ab major:

Ex. 21.20d

C#m7   E/F#   F#m7b5/B   D/E   Bm7/E   Amaj7   Am/B   B/E   Emaj7

E major:

2. *Construct the designated chords, voicing them either as triads or sevenths over a different bass note (if a triad over a different bass note is employed, double one of the members of the triad in order to always have four voices in the treble). Be sure to use good voice leading. Designate the chords with the simplest-to-read chord symbols.*

Ex. 21.21a

G major:

$Imaj9^{no3}$ $V9^{no5}_{sus4}$ V9sus4 $Imaj9^{no3}$

Ex. 21.21 b

C# minor:

V9sus4 $bVImaj9^{no3}$ bVII9sus4 $I7^{sus2}_{sus4}$ i

Ex. 21.21 c

Bb major:

$III9^{no5}_{sus4}$ IVmaj7 $V9^{no5}_{sus4}$ V7sus4(b9) $Imaj9^{no3}$

Chapter 22

Blues/Rock

Much of rock music is derived from blues harmony, blues melody, and blues form. The two most frequently used scales in traditional blues are pentatonic with an optional added chromatic note in each.

Ex. 22.1 Major Pentatonic

Ex. 22.2 Minor Pentatonic

Melodies using these scales are supported by harmonies that are usually either triads or dominant 7th-type chords. The 7th of the dominant 7th chords found in the blues progression are reflections of the tonal materials found in the blues scale.

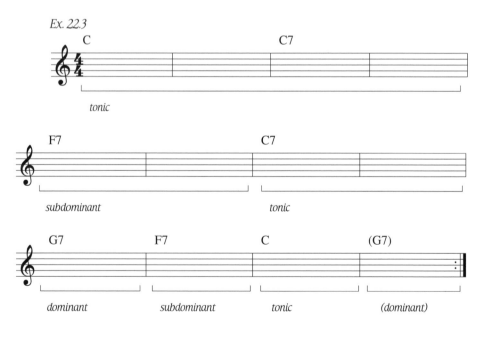

Ex. 22.3

154

independence of melody and harmony

Blues melody is more tonally independent from its harmony than either traditional major or minor melody is from its harmony. This independence is especially pronounced when the minor pentatonic melody sounds against the traditional diatonic major chords. Most characteristic is the clash of 3rds occurring between a minor 3rd melodically and a major 3rd harmonically. Blues usage also permits the perfect 4th above the root of the chord, usually a non-chord tone or a note that occurs with a chordal sus, to occur melodically over a triad or dominant 7th-type chord without having to resolve to a chord tone.

In the next example, the minor pentatonic scale is the tonal material used for the melody, whereas the harmony consists of all major chords or dominant 7th-type chords. The main commonality found between the melodic and the harmonic tonal materials is the tonal center (in this case, C). Notes marked with an asterisk (*) are simply blues scale tones which are not found in the harmony. They do not act the way non-chord tones in traditional major/minor act (i.e., non-chord tones in traditional major/minor tend to resolve to a member of the sustained harmony); rather, they act independently, following their own melodic tone tendencies, not the dictates of the sustained harmony. The dissonances resulting from the clashes between melody and harmony are, in fact, one of the most important aspects in defining the music as blues.

Ex. 22.4

The two blues pentatonic scales are often found within the same 12-bar pattern. The combined notes of the two pentatonic scales plus their optional chromatic tones produce a more complete blues scale.

Ex. 22.5

The following example shows the use of both pentatonic scale forms in the melody:

Ex. 22.6

characteristic rock harmony   The minor pentatonic harmonized entirely with major triads retains the characteristic bluesy clashing 3rds within a purely harmonic framework.

Ex. 22.7

root motion   The root motion of these triads, which were originally treated as "thickened melody," is significant. Movement up or down a minor 3rd and down a major 2nd are common root movements in rock music.

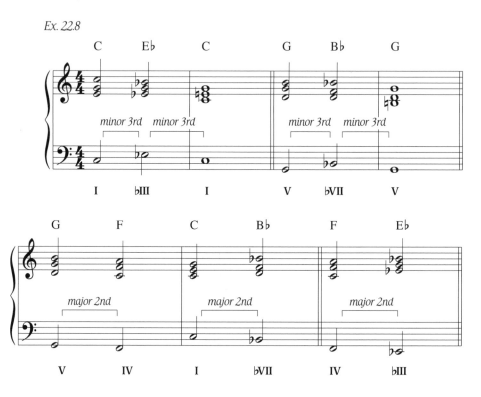

Ex. 22.8

In addition, the root movement down a perfect 4th is very prevalent in rock music.

Ex. 22.9

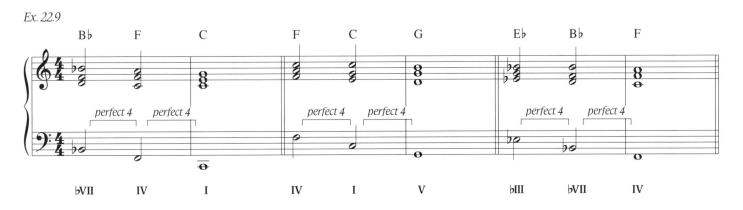

The ♭VI chord, derived from the parallel natural minor mode (modal interchange), is also frequently used. It creates the bluesy clash of 3rds when it precedes or follows the IV chord. (This clash of major and minor 3rds in adjacent chords is referred to as "cross relations" in traditional harmony texts.) The II chord moving to the IV chord also creates the characteristic hallmark of clashing 3rds.

Ex. 22.10

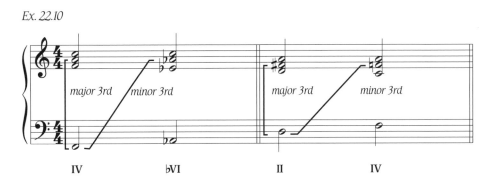

"Addicted to Love"

The melody in the chorus of this rock classic consists of a repeated two-measure phrase that uses either the major or minor 3rd of the key, a common melodic gesture found in blues. The harmony is provided by power chords built on some of the roots of the A minor pentatonic scale (C and E are missing). Root motion characteristic of rock occurs: down a major 2nd and down a perfect 4th.

Addicted to Love

Words and Music by
Robert Palmer

form in blues and early rock Traditional blues is made up of three four-measure phrases. The lyric structure for each four measures is *aab* It is a deceptively simple form. Its three phrases define it as an asymmetric structure. (This may partially account for the fact that you can play the blues all night long without tiring of it.) There are three areas that are points of harmonic and phrasal emphasis and are, therefore, possible placement areas for the central statement (title, hook) in the blues form.

emphasis at the beginning (measure 1)

The central statement (title, hook) often appears immediately, especially if the traditional blues lyric structure is used. In the traditional blues lyric structure using a rhymed couplet, the first line (*a*) repeated by the second line (*a*) and then rhymed in the third line (*b*), allows the title to be repeated at least twice.

The traditional form has often been incorporated into more contemporary song forms, such as the verse/chorus song form. In order for it to work as a verse/chorus song form (in this case, chorus/verse form), the first statement, lyrically and musically, has to be recapitulated. The lyric for the next section, the verse section, usually contains more lines (and musical phrases) in order to tell the story and provides a contrast to the chorus with both a rhythmic and a phrasal acceleration.

Ex. 21.12

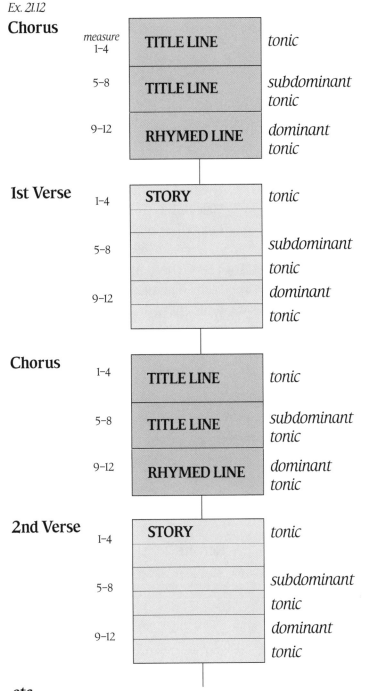

etc.

This form is found in many early rock hits, such as Chuck Berry's "Maybellene."

159

emphasis at the subdominant (measure 5)

The I7 chord (containing the tritone) is a tension-building device. Its point of arrival is the IV chord and for that reason the IV or IV7 acts as a natural place to hang the central statement (title, hook). Frequently, early rock and roll hits further emphasized the tension-building quality of the I7 chord by using a stop time rhythm on the first quarter-note of the first four bars. The resulting song form, a short verse with a longer chorus, takes place entirely within 12 bars.

Ex. 22.13

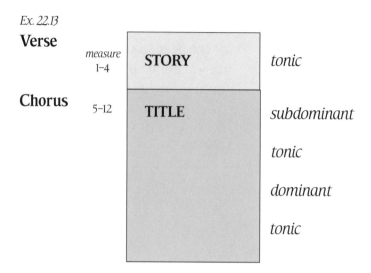

Good examples of this particular structuring of the blues form is Bill Haley's hit, "Rock Around the Clock" written by Max Freedman and Jimmy DeKnight, and Carl Perkins' equally famous "Blue Suede Shoes."

emphasis on the dominant (measure 9) or on the final cadence

The V chord in measure 9 is the beginning of the last section of the blues. The title may appear right on the V chord or it may appear on the tonic chord at measure 11. The return to the tonic can be very satisfying and can be used to hang the central statement (title, hook). The resulting song form is a verse/refrain.

Ex. 22.14

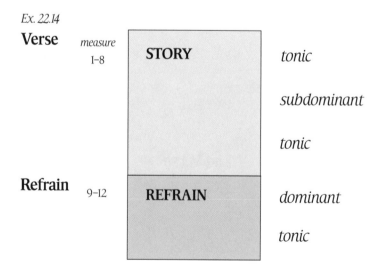

Early rock hits such as Chuck Berry's "Back In the USA" and "Roll Over Beethoven" are examples using this structure.

adding a bridge to the blues
Early writers of rock songs went one step further by adding a bridge as a contrasting section after two repetitions of the blues format, resulting in an *AABA* song form.

Ex. 22.15

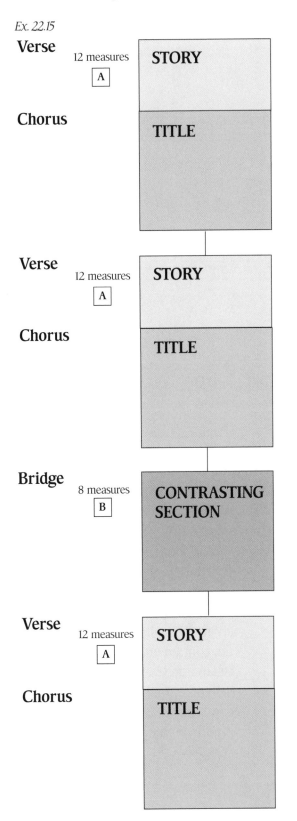

Verse — 12 measures — A — STORY

Chorus — TITLE

Verse — 12 measures — A — STORY

Chorus — TITLE

Bridge — 8 measures — B — CONTRASTING SECTION

Verse — 12 measures — A — STORY

Chorus — TITLE

This format is found in Lieber and Stoller's humorous blues/rock song, "Charlie Brown."

other blues-derived forms

There are numerous ways to expand (or contract) all of the above structures. One of the most common is the simple doubling of the measures, thereby producing a 24-bar structure.

Any of the harmonic functions can be elongated or even repeated. The structure found in Ex. 22.15 is 20 measures long but certainly is a recognizably blues-derived form.

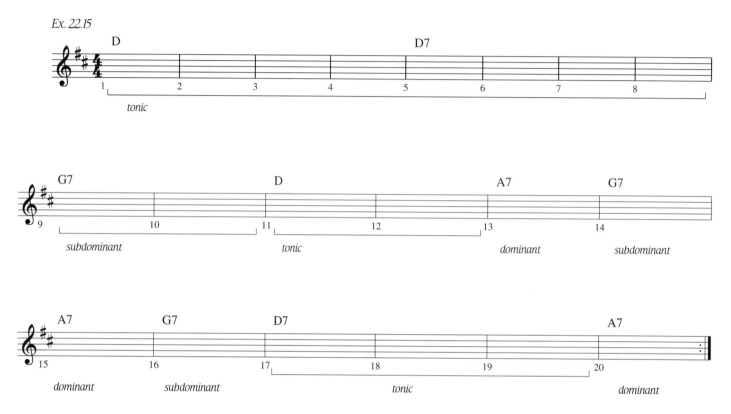

Ex. 22.15

Many rock and R&B songs take just a couple of blues-derived harmonic devices and build entire song structures from them. To cite one example, Otis Redding's "Respect" repeats the move from V to IV throughout the entire verse, finally arriving on the tonic chord with the title and hook of the song.

stylistic considerations

Open 5th structures are very common in rock music. These "power chords," usually sounded on highly amplified guitars in a fairly low register, contain only the root and perfect 5th of the triad, allowing for either the major 3rd or minor 3rd to be sung or played with them. Instrumental riffs are endemic to this music, and many rock songs are constructed starting from an instrumental riff. The vocal melody, which is added later, acts as a counterline or counterpoint to the riff.

Ex. 22.17

* sound *8va* lower

assignment   *Compose a rock song—melody, chords, title (lyric optional)—that is not strictly a blues, but uses the blues form as a point of departure and also uses the various scales and harmonies derived from the blues. Choose a point in the form for the placement of the central statement. Identify where the central statement occurs and identify the form you have chosen (verse/chorus; verse/refrain; AABA or other).*

163

Chapter 23

Modes

Use of modes in popular songs, especially R&B, rock, pop, and folk-derived styles, is widespread. There are a couple of reasons why modes are sometimes chosen as basic tonal materials rather than the traditional major/minor scales. First, traditional major/minor scales, though still viable, have been fully explored in the popular song arena for a long time and offer few surprises. Modes can sound fresh—depending on their treatment. Modes can be, and often are, used in conjunction with traditional major/minor. Second, modality works very well in creating dance music or any groove-oriented music. One of the objectives in dance music is to create a steady, almost hypnotic groove. In groove-oriented music, it is important that the music doesn't noticeably cadence too often; otherwise, a stop-go effect results. Most modes (all except the Lydian) don't contain a leading tone which is one of the main characteristics of traditional major/minor and one of the main factors in creating strong cadences. The lack of strong cadential potential in modes is a positive feature when viewed in this context.

Aeolian mode or natural minor

The Aeolian, Dorian, and Mixolydian modes are the most widely used modes in present-day popular music and for this reason are the only ones presented in this chapter.

Ex. 23.1 Characteristic Scale Degrees of the Aeolian Mode

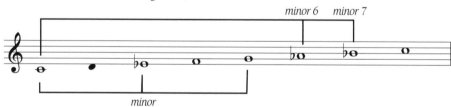

Ex. 23.2 Stability/Instability of the Scale Degrees in the Aeolian Mode

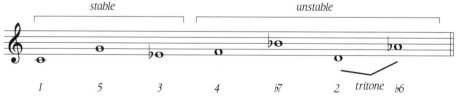

Ex. 23.3 Tone Tendencies of the Aeolian Mode

The 2nd degree and the 6th degree are the most unstable degrees of the Aeolian mode because of their half-step relationship to the nearest stable tones and because they form the interval of a tritone.

Modal melodies function in the same fashion as melodies found in the traditional major and minor system in that unstable tones tend to resolve to stable tones. Melodic tonal implications are an important factor in creating a strong sense of tonality in a chosen mode.

If the melody implies a strong 5–1 or 3–1 relationship, a strong sense of tonality can be established.

Ex. 23.4a

Note how the example below implies E♭ major rather than C Aeolian.

Ex. 23.4b

Melodic cadences on stable tones—especially the tonic—help establish the tonal center. Study the following melody, especially noticing:

(1) The melodic cadences and (2)The resolution of the unstable tones.

Ex. 23.5

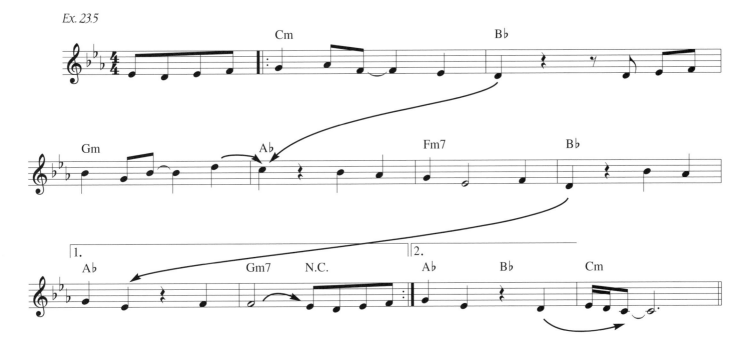

Ex. 23.6 Diatonic Triads and 7th Chords of the Aeolian Mode

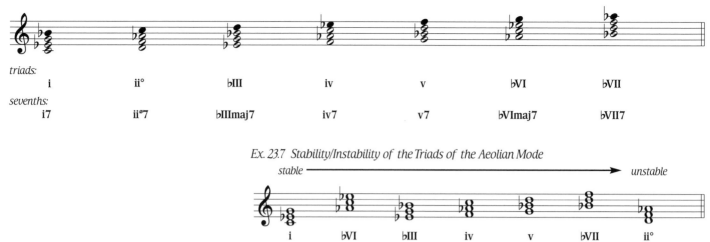

triads:
    i   ii°   ♭III   iv   v   ♭VI   ♭VII

sevenths:
    i7   ii°7   ♭IIImaj7   iv7   v7   ♭VImaj7   ♭VII7

Ex. 23.7 Stability/Instability of the Triads of the Aeolian Mode

stable ⟶ unstable

    i   ♭VI   ♭III   iv   v   ♭VII   ii°

chord progressions in the Aolian mode

Chord progressions in modal music have characteristics that differentiate them from chord progressions in traditional major/minor. The Aeolian mode has no leading tone; therefore, the dominant is considerably weakened. The v, while an unstable triad, is no more unstable than either the ii° and the ♭VII. Both ♭VII and ii°7 in traditional harmony are considered subdominants, but in the context of the Aeolian mode, they have more characteristics associated with the dominant function—they are very unstable and tend to resolve to the tonic.

strong cadencing progressions

Although modal music has less of a tendency to cadence due to the lack of a leading tone, there are times when establishing a strong sense of tonality is needed and desired. The following progressions help establish a tonal center in the Aeolian mode. Notice that the tonic chord is always placed in a strong cadential position.

A strong cadencing chord is ♭VII, a major triad, which provides a strong root/bass movement up a major second to the tonic chord.

The ♭VI–♭VII–i progression is very strong, with root movements up in major seconds.

Ex. 23.8

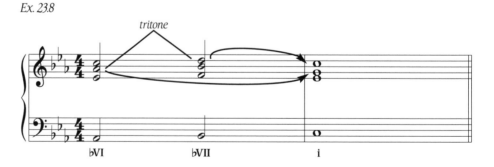

    ♭VI   ♭VII   i

Equally strong is ♭VI–v–i. A strong cadence is still provided by iv–v–i.

Ex. 23.9

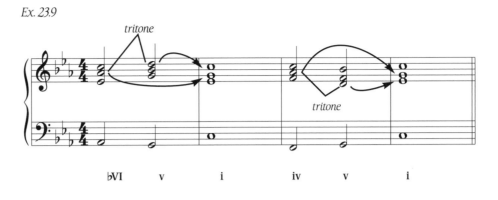

♭VI   v   i   iv   v   i

As illustrated in the preceding examples, any two consecutive triads that contain a tritone form a strong cadencing progression.

The resolution of the two tones that make up the tritone causes a very strong resolution to the triad built on the ♭3 scale degree and allows the Aeolian to modulate easily to the relative major (the major key built on the ♭III). The tones of the tritone are unstable tones that find resolution in stable tones both in the key of Aeolian minor and its relative major.

Ex. 23.10

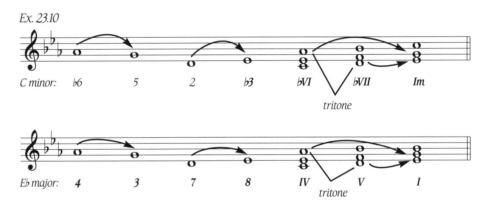

C minor: ♭6   5   2   ♭3   ♭VI   ♭VII   Im   *tritone*

E♭ major: 4   3   7   8   IV   V   I   *tritone*

The ability of the Aeolian minor to easily move to the relative major shouldn't be considered a liability. Rather, it should be considered another option.

root motion   One of the benefits in using modes is the greater choice of root motion. Common root motions found in traditional major/minor are a perfect 5th down, diminished 5th up or down, major or minor 3rds down, major 2nd up, and minor 2nd up or down. Characteristic root motion found in modal music varies according to the mode. Root motion includes those listed with traditional major/minor but also contains root motion generally not found in traditional major/minor, for instance, down a major 2nd or up a minor 3rd.

The following examples of progressions in the Aeolian mode were culled from hit songs. The root motion is indicated below the progressions.

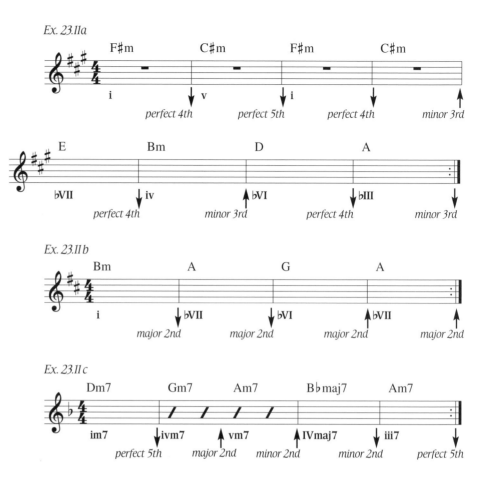

Ex. 23.11a

Ex. 23.11b

Ex. 23.11c

When composing with modes, keep in mind these factors that help establish a sense of harmonic progression:

1. The least noticeable change in consecutive chords in a progression is achieved by changing only one member of the harmony. The greatest noticeable change in consecutive chords in a progression is achieved by changing all three notes.

2. The more stable tones a harmony possesses, the more stable it will be; the fewer it has, the less stable it will be. A progression from least stable to most stable (or vice versa) will provide the most noticeable change.

Ex. 23.12

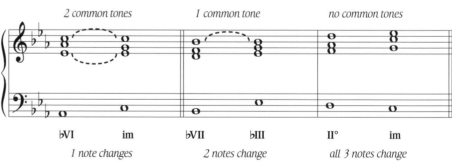

writing tip If you have trouble making harmonic choices in modal music, try practicing diatonic modal progressions on a daily basis until their sounds become part of your working vocabulary.

Dorian mode The Dorian mode is a minor mode with a characteristic major 6th scale degree.

Ex. 23.13 Characteristic Scale Degrees of the Dorian Mode

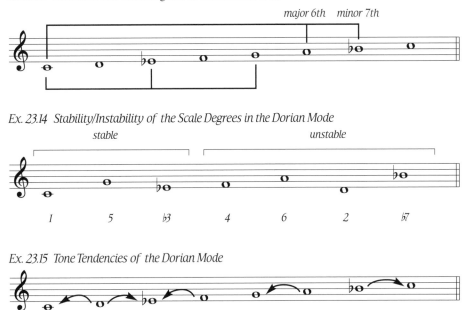

Ex. 23.14 Stability/Instability of the Scale Degrees in the Dorian Mode

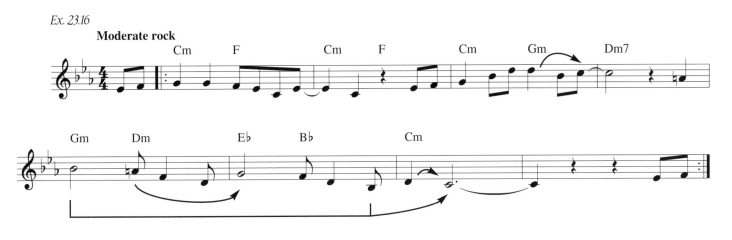

Ex. 23.15 Tone Tendencies of the Dorian Mode

Study the following melody and harmonic progression, especially noticing (1) the melodic cadences, (2) the resolution of the unstable tones, and (3) the root motion of the chord progression.

Ex. 23.16

Moderate rock

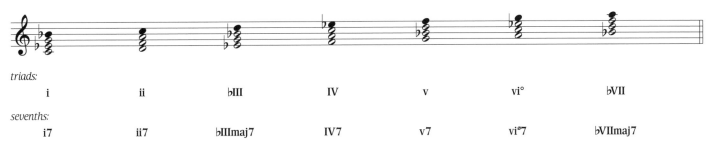

Ex. 23.17 Diatonic Triads and 7ths of the Dorian Mode

triads:

i	ii	♭III	IV	v	vi°	♭VII

sevenths:

i7	ii7	♭IIImaj7	IV7	v7	vi°7	♭VIImaj7

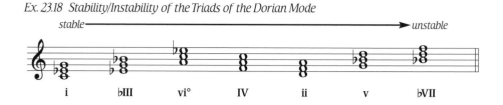

Ex. 23.18 *Stability/Instability of the Triads of the Dorian Mode*

stable ──────────────────────────────────→ unstable

i   ♭III   vi°   IV   ii   v   ♭VII

The vi°, an unstable triad by its very nature (a diminished chord contains a tritone rather than a perfect 5th), is rated fairly stable to the tonality because it contains the tonic and ♭3 degree, both stable tones. The close relationship between the tonic chord and vi° can more easily be grasped when a 7th is added to VI°, providing three common tones between vi7(♭5) and the tonic chord.

The tritone in a traditional harmonic context as well as in the Aeolian mode creates strong cadential progressions to the tonic. In the Dorian mode, however, one of the members of the tritone—the 3rd degree of the mode—is a stable tone! This makes it more difficult to create a strong harmonic cadence in the Dorian mode than in the previous scales we have examined. The 6th scale degree of the Dorian mode is not often used melodically in popular songs because of its tritonic relationship to the stable 3rd degree. It is rather difficult to hear and to sing the 6th scale degree, but this should not dissuade you from using it altogether. (It certainly does not dissuade Sting, who uses it frequently).

Ex. 23.19

chord progressions in the Dorian mode

The most characteristic scale degree of the Dorian mode is the major 6th degree. A chord progression from the tonic chord to IV or the tonic chord to ii gives an instant Dorian sound to a progression (IV and ii both contain the major 6th scale degree). Although it is more difficult to set up a strong cadential progression in the Dorian mode than in the Aeolian mode, the following are examples of progressions that do establish the Dorian tonic:

Ex. 23.20

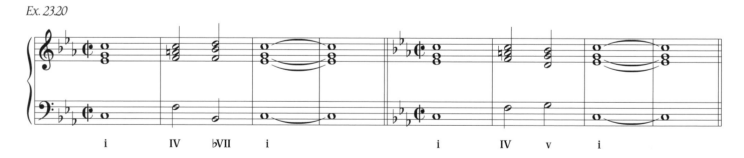

i   IV   ♭VII   i   i   IV   v   i

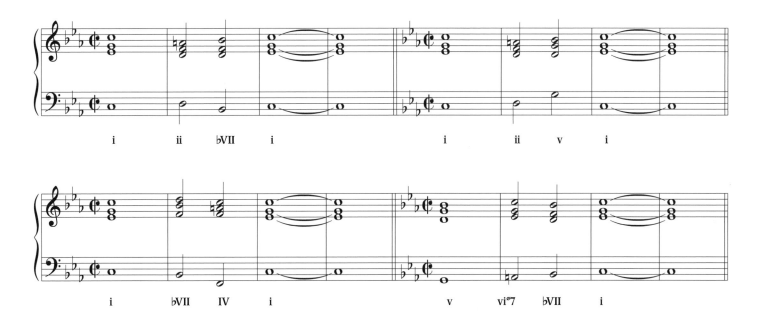

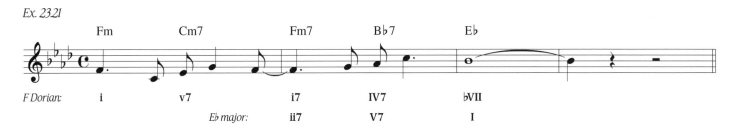

Because of the placement of the tritone within the mode (the 3rd degree, one of its members, is a stable tone), the Dorian mode can easily modulate to a major key that has its tonic built on the Dorian ♭7 scale degree. You have probably learned that the major key a minor 3rd above a minor key is its relative major. This is true for all traditional minor scales and for the Aeolian mode, but it is not true for the rest of the modes. The relative major for the Dorian mode (the major key containing the same set of tones as those found in the Dorian mode) is found a major 2nd below the Dorian tonic.

The ability of the Dorian minor to easily move to its relative major shouldn't be considered a liability; it should be considered another option.

Ex. 23.21

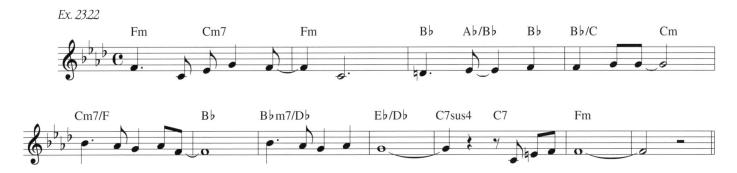

Very few popular songs are written entirely in the Dorian mode. Since the Dorian mode does present fairly resistant cadential possibilities, another minor scale may be employed in conjunction with it. It is not uncommon for a song to begin in the Dorian mode and change to Aeolian mode or even to introduce the leading tone (borrowed from melodic minor ascending) at an important cadence.

Ex. 23.22

Mixolydian mode   The Mixolydian mode is a major mode with a ♭7 instead of the leading tone found in the traditional major scale.

Ex. 23.23 Characteristic Scale Degrees of the Mixolydian Mode

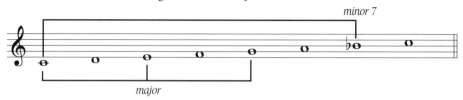

Ex. 23.24 Stability/Instability of the Scale Degrees in the Mixolydian Mode

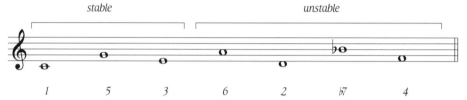

Ex. 23.25 Tone Tendencies of the Mixolydian Mode

Study the following melody and chord progression, especially noticing (1) the melodic cadences, (2) the resolution of the unstable tones, and (3) the root motion of the chord progression.

Ex. 23.26 B♭ Mixolydian

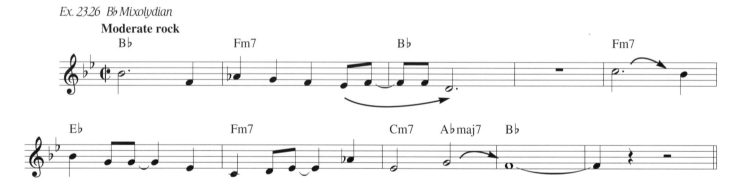

Ex. 23.27 Diatonic Triads and 7ths in the Mixolydian Mode

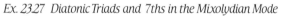

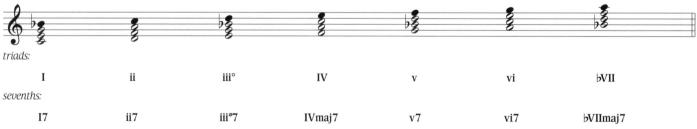

triads:						
I	ii	iii°	IV	v	vi	♭VII

sevenths:						
I7	ii7	iii°7	IVmaj7	v7	vi7	♭VIImaj7

Ex. 23.28 Stability/Instability of the Triads of the Mixolydian Mode

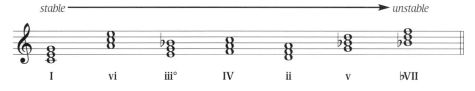

The difference of one note between the traditional major scale and the Mixolydian mode is extremely important not only because the Mixolydian mode no longer has a leading tone, but also because its tritone is now located in a very different place from its location in the traditional major scale.

The tritone in the Mixolydian mode is formed by the ♭7th degree and the stable 3rd degree.

Ex. 23.29

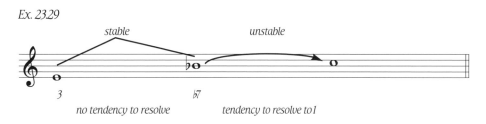

It is, therefore, fairly difficult to create a strong harmonic cadence to the Mixolydian tonic. There is also a strong tendency for the I chord or the V7/IV chord in Mixolydian to take on a dominant function to a new tonic in traditional major built on the Mixolydian 4th scale degree.

Ex. 23.30

typical Mixolydian progressions The ♭VII chord is the most frequently employed chord when creating a strong cadence to the Mixolydian tonic. The following examples have been culled from hit songs:

Ex. 23.31a

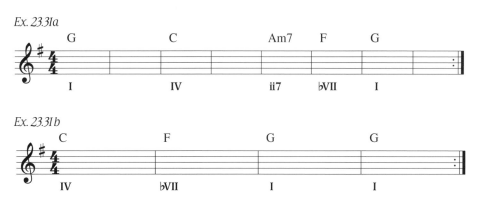

Ex. 23.31b

173

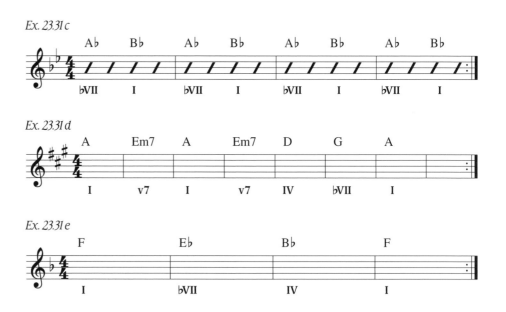

Ex. 23.31 c

Ex. 23.31 d

Ex. 23.31 e

use of pedal point   One device frequently used in modal writing in order to anchor the tonality is a tonic pedal point.

Ex. 23.32

assignment   1. *Write a section of a song (8–16 measures) in the Aeolian mode. Indicate root motion for each progression.*

2. *Write a section of a song (8–16 measures) in the Dorian mode.*

3. *Write a section of a song (8–16 measures) in the Mixolydian mode. Use a tonic pedal tone throughout. All of the above sections should include melody, chords, and tempo/groove indication.*

The purpose of this assignment is to familiarize you in a personal and creative way with the sound and workings of each of these modes. Continue to experiment with each of these modes until they become part of your vocabulary.

Afterword

The tools and techniques presented to you in this book are an important part of the essential musical knowledge needed by aspiring songwriters. Topics that need exposition or further exploration are writing from a groove, bass line or riff; refinements in setting lyrics; and the many implications of prosody.

Songwriting strategies and how to use tonality in form (such as modulation, polymodality) are topics that demand another book. Understanding various song styles and writing in those styles is a subject that could also constitute the contents of another book.

The joy of songwriting comes in creating an entity containing no superfluous note or word—a crystalline gem that touches others. My hope is that this book has helped you move closer to that joy.

Biography

Jack Perricone's distinguished career as songwriter, composer and arranger includes such hits as "Run, Joey, Run," which reached *Billboard's 1975 Top Five*, and Angela Bofill's, "What I Wouldn't Do." His songs have appeared on the pop, R&B, and country charts and have been recorded by Lou Rawls, Jerry Butler, K.T. Oslin and many others. His numerous credits as record producer include a Grammy-nominated jazz album and a recent Gail Wynters' album, *Boogie to Heaven*, featuring Dr. John.

Jack Perricone co-founded Berklee College of Music's unique Songwriting Department, which he has chaired since 1987.

Index